Stages in Development Thinking and Emerging Challenges for Development Economics

Stages in Development Thinking and Emerging Challenges for Development Economics

G.P. Isser

BOOKWELL
NEW DELHI

First Edition 2000

ISBN: 81-85040-38-9

Published by:

BOOKWELL

Sales Office

24/4800, Ansari Road,
Darya Ganj, New Delhi-110002
Ph: 91-11-3268786, 3257264

Head Office:

2/72, Nirankari Colony,
Delhi-110009
Ph: 91-11-7251283
FAX: 91-11-3281315
E-mail: bkwell@nde.vsnl.net.in

Computer Typesetting and cover designed by:
Ghanshyam Das Kushwaha

Printed in India by:

DP's Impressive Impressions,
New Delhi-110059. Ph: 5642897

For Godavari

Contents

List of Tables

Preface

The birth of development economics in the postwar era was a manifestation of human faith in the capacity of the man to harness human resources, science and technology to raise the standard of the poor and thereby narrow the gap between rich and poor within the nations, on the one hand and between rich and poor nations on the other hand. A separate body of economic thought to deal with specific problem of economic development had its origin in the postwar consensus that the limits on the creation of wealth in the classical economic thought could not be sustained on empirical evidence of a long era of global economic prosperity. The poverty in the world existed not because the economic growth had inevitable limits as visualised by classical economists David Ricardo, T.R. Malthus and J.S. Mill but because the problem of developing poor nations could not be comprehended and analysed on the basis of the postulates of conventional economic theories which were founded on the neoclassical concepts.

The emerging consensus was that through the development process, the developing countries will catch up with rich and industrialised nations and the poverty will be wiped out from the globe. While a small number of countries have graduated from the state of under development, for the majority of nations, development continues to remain a distant goal. The global economy today witnesses a widening development gap between rich and poor nations. Alongwith this dichotomy, the growing number of poor inhabiting the developing world who remain on the edge of survival, present a formidable challenge to development thought and policy.

On the one hand, technology has accelerated advance towards globalisation and integration in the world economy and on the other hand, a number of developing countries have become marginalised. The growing deprivation and poverty in a number of developing countries amidst the rising wave of globalisation calls for an urgent analysis of the various aspects of development economics. The book analyses the body of thought which has provided policy orientation to developing countries and examines the various stages through which development economics has undergone.

One of the lessons of development experience is that the neoclassical resurgence in development theorising which came as a counter-revolution to development economics, could not fully meet the challenge of narrowing development gap. Reliance on the dictum 'Get the prices right' had limited impact on development in a number of countries.

The recent crisis in some of the East Asian economies demonstrated that the policy of depending on market forces has its limitations. The lessons of East Asian crisis bring us back to the need for a theoretical framework within which economic policy takes into account advantages of an open economy and the imbalances that this can bring out in an economy.

Poverty alleviation has emerged as a major challenge for development economics. Neither planned economic development which was based on orthodox development theory nor neo-liberal development strategy relying on market forces could meet the challenge. For meeting this challenge, the most important task will be to provide a very strong empirical support to.theoretical framework of development economics which will lead to differentiated development strategies for national economic development. The developing countries are highly differentiated in the characteristics of underdevelopment and in this regard it is through intensive empirical research rather than through theoretical models that the growth effective policies can be launched.

In course of last four decades the structure and pattern of global economy has undergone profound changes. This has generated new debates on the concepts embodied in the writings of pioneers of development economics such as Ragnar Nurkse, W.W. Rostow, Raul Prebisch, Gunnar Myrdal. The classic centre-periphery relationship in which the developing nations supplied primary commodities to the industrialised countries in exchange for the manufactured goods has only limited applicability in a new global division of labour. International Trade is no longer influenced only by the centre-periphery relations which were cornerstone of development theory of Raul Prebisch, Myrdal and Hans singer. Several other economic forces influence trade relations.

Similarly the applicability of the theory of comparative advantage of nations in International Trade has become limited as a result of increasing production capacity of the third world and global sourcing of production. The globalisation and open International Trade has encouraged nations to specialise in different branches of manufacturing and production capacity is dispersed among a number of developed and developing countries depending on the stage of production.

The challenge for development economics is to enrich its analytical tools and address to new problems which the developing countries face in their endeavour to attack underdevelopment and poverty. The belief that the efficiency of market economy in bringing out rapid growth in some developing economies will eventually result in the decline of development economics ignores the persistence of widening development gap among nations which will need the intellectual support and analysis provided by the mainstream development economics.

Development Economics which had its origin in postwar era has come of age. In its long journey during the last four decades, fast changing developments in global economy leading to neoclassical resurgence in development thought, generated intensive debates on the survival of development economics as a separate branch of discipline. The basic strand of thought which underlines analytical framework of my book is that development economics, will continue to be valid till the poverty in the developing world persists and so long, the gap between rich and poor nations continues to widen. I have found it very difficult to support the school of thought which maintains that conventional economics provides adequate theoretical framework for analysing the problem of economic development in the developing world. The message that the book conveys to readers is that to meet the challenge of poverty eradication and rapid convergence of developing countries with the developed world, the analytical framework provided by development economics is relevant and to meet new challenges of development, it has to evolve in new directions.

For an urgent attack on poverty, innovations in theoretical and policy framework of development economics are required. For poverty alleviation both growth and appropriate policy orientation to increase the income of the poor is required. It is imperative that development economics concentrates on areas of research which identify obstacles to poverty elimination. The area of research which needs to be given priority is to study policies for the creation of employment opportunities for the poor by overcoming constraints of inadequate investible resources.

Poverty in third world is both a moral and intellectual challenge. The deprivation suffered by poor people call for an urgent attack on poverty in the developing world. Towards this direction, development economics has to extend strong intellectual support to the necessity and desirability of poverty eradication. My contention in this context is that removal of poverty is not only a moral imperative but is also a sound economic proposition. The existence of widespread poverty in developing economy dampens the demand for goods and services on the one hand and results in loss to wealth of nations in terms of idle human resources on the other hand. The concept that I would like to expound through this book, is that removal of poverty should be treated as an input to the generation of income in the developing economy and investment in utilising idle manpower should be given priority in the development strategy of developing countries.

In writing this book, one of the major constraints was access to current and uptodate documents and reference materials on development economics which has most dynamic and ever-changing parameters. Before I conclude preface to the book, I wish to express appreciation for those who helped me in this regard.

First and foremost, I owe a debt of gratitude to Dr.V.R. Panchamukhi, Director General of Research and Information System for the Non-Aligned and other developing Countries (R.I.S.) for extending facilities of consultation and study in R.I.S. library which has a remarkable collection of books on development issues. I would like to extend my special thanks to Sh. V.K. Jain, Director, (Library), Ministry of External Affairs, and to the Librarian of National Council of Applied Economic Research (NCAER) for facilitating study and research work. They extended excellent cooperation to me in my present endeavour.

In course of analysing development experience of the developing economies especially of the Least Developed Countries, I have extensively drawn on the various issues of the Trade and Development Report, published by UNCTAD Secretariat. I owe special words of grateful thanks to the secretary General of UNCTAD.

Finally, in writing the book, I have been greatly benefited by the writings of development economists and I express my gratitude to all of them.

G.P. ISSER

1

Introduction

Economists through ages have done great service to the mankind through their thinking on various aspects of economic growth. Since the publication of "Wealth of Nations" in 1776, a number of theories and concepts were developed to provide analytical tools for examining ways and means to create wealth. The perception of economists on economic development have been changing in tune with changing phases in the history of world economy. The evolution of economic thought was also influenced by the current of political, economic and social developments in the global economy both at national and at international level.

Against the background of trends in global economy, it has become important to survey the development thought of the economists and to examine how the changing international economic scenario reflects the rationale and validity of the theories and concepts of the great thinkers on development issues. Alongwith a broad canvas on the history of development thinking since classical era, the book surveys the recent development experience of the third world and examines how the development economics should evolve in future to address the major problems of povery-alleviation and widening development gap.

Early development thinking was largely influenced by classical economists. For the classical economists the long term growth was an important area of inquriy. Chapter Two briefly surveys the contributions of Adam Smith, David Ricardo, T.R. Malthus and J.S. Mill and Karl Marx in Classical tradition and also surveys contributions by economists such as schumpeter and Keynes who influenced development thinking. In analysing the economic thought of these economists, effort has been made to segregate the concepts relevant to the analysis of growth theory in various historical phases. Since the aim of the book is to analyse the development thought and development experience, the historical survey is precise and very selective. There is no attempt to elaborate vast mass of theories expounded by these economists.

The idea of economic growth was foremost in the thoughts of economists till 1870 when marginal revolution took place in the history of economic thought. The neoclassical economists relegated the concept of macro economic growth to the background and concentrated on micro analysis. Because of continued economic growth in later part of 19th century resulting from industrial and technological progress, the pessimistic vision of the classicals, of economy returning to stationary state no longer caused concern to the economists. They attached importance to efficient allocation of resources rather than to the creation of wealth. In neoclassical economics, the economic functioning of entities such as production, distribution and prices were explained in terms of rational individual self-interest. Marginalism as expounded by Jevons, Walras, Manger was key to the determination of values, distribution and utility. With marginalism a new approach to economics developed.

Micro analysis dominated the economic thought till Joseph Schumpeter appeared on the scene in 1911. Schumpeter made significant contributions to the evolution of development thinking and in this respect broke with basic postulates of classical growth theories as it was perceived by Adam Smith, Ricardo, Mathus, Marx, and J.S. Mill.

For Schumpeter it is not mobilisation of savings, which is crucial for development, but it is entrepreneur who combines the factors of production in new ways through innovation that increases productivity. Development in Schumpeter's view is the result of new combination which is made by an entrepreneur either through the introduction of a new product or through a new method of production or through opening of a new market. Schumpeter's great contribution to the history of development thinking was that he brought growth-analysis to the centre-stage which was eclipsed for several decades after J.S. Mill's publication of 'Principles of Political Economy', in 1848.

In 1930's the keynesian revolution influenced the thinking on development. Keynes presented the analysis of output, investment and employment in aggregative terms and the macro approach of Keynes later proved very useful and effective tool in growth -analysis. Keynes's major contribution to economic thought was its break from the classical orthodoxy that under competitive conditions resources will be fully employed.

Keynesian theory gave a background to the analytical framework for development analysis which dominated economic thought in the postwar era. Keynes had expounded the theory that it was possible for an economy to run down and fail to generate sufficiently high level of activity to avoid involuntary unemployment. This was basic to the analysis of economic variables in developing economies because it was the possibility of disequilibrium in the economy that represented basic perspectives of development economics later The influence of Keynes on development economics also came through post keynesian growth-analysis especially the formulation of Harrod-Domar Model which brought the issues of development to the forefront of economists's agenda.

The postwar affluence in north and its awareness in developing countries convinced the mankind that poverty is not inevitable. The global economic scenario reflected growing gaps in incomes between poor South and rich North. The neoclassical paradigms with its reliance on market forces in global production and distribution did not confirm to new realities. The 1950s represented a watershed in the evolution of development economics. The economists of the postwar era shifted their attention to the investigation of the causes of poverty in underdeveloped countries and suggested policy measures to overcome it. This paved the way for the emergence of development economics as a separate branch of study from the mainstream economics. To address the problems of economic development, the economists developed new theoretical framework embodying new concepts and tools which could analyse the causes of widespread povery and underdevelopment in the large part of the globe spanning Asia, Africa and Latin America.

The development economics in 1950s and 1960s developed new theories to encompass specific problems of developing countries such as underemployment and lack of capital, overpopulation. Immediately preceding this new intellectual thrust, Keynesian attack on orthodox economics had provided a stimulus for analysing economies operating at less than full employment level. Those who contributed towards the new thinking on development included the pioneers such as W.A. Lewis, R. Nurkse, W.W. Rostow, Gunnar Myrdal, Raul Prebisch, Rosenstein Rodan etc.

These pioneers brought the goal of economic development to the attention of national and international policy makers. The economists differed on the development perspectives. W.W. Rostow developed stage theory of economic development. He stressed that all societies must pass through five stages in growth process; the traditional society, the preconditions for take off, the take off, the drive to maturity and to the age of mass consumption. W.A. Lewis, emphasised on the role of capital accumulation in economic growth and developed dualistic model of economic growth. Paul Rosenstein Rodan developed the strategy of "Big Push" through public policy which could overcome limitations of market in initiating growth in developing countries. His thesis of `Big Push' was based on the necessity of large infrastructural investment necessary for industrialisation which market could not ensure.

In 1963, Dudley Seers categorically rejected the claim of economic theory that it had universal validity. He stated that the theory was only valid in a special case namely that of modern industrial capitalism. In his essay which was published in 1963, he said, "Economists seem very much slow in adapting themselves to the requirements of the main task of the day: the elimination of acute poverty in Asia, Africa and Latin America." Seer's thesis was one of the basic foundations of development economics and especially for further evolution of structuralist school of thought in development thinking.

Some economists in Marxist tradition argued that the forces which led to development in industrialised countries also led to underdevelopment in the developing countries. Andre Gunder Frank, one of the founders of neo-marxist interpretation of economic development thought that the state of underdevelopment in poor countries resulted from the exploitation by the developed countries.

In Gunnar Myrdal's theory of economic development, there was a conceptual evolution of link between economic growth and equality. He held the view that equalisation in favour of the lower income is a productive investment in the quality of people and that higher consumption levels in Myrdal's theory of development was a necessary condition for more stable and rapid economic growth. In `Asian Drama' and later in the `Challenge of World Poverty'. He adhered to the view that egalitarian institutional reforms to raise the competitive level of the poor would lead to more rapid economic growth.

R. Nurkse developed several concepts of economic growth in his book `Problems of Capital Formation in Underdeveloped Countries'. He expounded the theory of vicious circle of low income, low savings, low investment, low income which had to be broken for initiating growth process in developing economies. He also analysed the phenomenon of `Disguised Unemployment' in the developing economies which created obstacle to development and because of low savings, it proved to be a source of bottleneck in crossing this hurdle. Nurkse also expounded the concepts of `Balanced Growth' for economic development.

By late 1960s and by early 1970s, mass of development literature with numerous growth theories and models were brought out by economists from all regions. As development economics matured and came of age, the focus in development economics shifted from growth models to the study and analysis of development experience of developing countries who were in various stages of industrialisation. The investigations showed that the development experience was heterogeneous and diverse. The postulates of development economics came to close scrutiny and the effectiveness of development policies based on theoretical models of development economics in the attainment of growth targets was questioned.

In late 1960s, a trend towards neoclassicism surfaced in development thinking. One of the offshoots of new thinking among economists was renewed emphasis on the interaction between trade and development. The economists became more pre-occupied with debate on the role of trade and trade was elevated as engine of growth in the development literature in 1970s and in 1980s. The rapid economic growth of newly industrialised economies in East Asia and the wave of liberalisation and openness in trade and investment in various parts of the world further consolidated the neoclassical resurgence in development thinking.

Since 1970, the analysis of factors contributing to divergence in growth performance dominated development literature. This necessitated detailed country studies and the international development institutions both within the UN system and outside played a decisive role in sponsoring these studies. The factors affecting economic development in developing world were so numerous and heterogeneous that generalised development theories had very limited validity.

As pointed out earlier with the onset of 1970s, the content of development analysis had undergone substantial changes. The empirical evidence of cross-country growth experience showed that policies both domestic and external, oriented towards market economy achieved higher rate of economic growth in comparison with those developing economies who had controlled economic system. The neoclassical resurgence in development thinking called for structural adjustment policies, liberalisation and privatisation. The thinking among economists evolved towards this direction and that was later known as `Washington Consensus.' The expectation of the economists was that the implementation of policies based on Washington

Consensus would enable developing economies to integrate with the world economy and the integration would further enable them to `catch up' with the developed countries.

Alongwith the neoclassical resurgence, the eighties witnessed mounting theoretical attacks on the basic tenets of the development economics. In an essay entitled `The Rise and Fall of Development Economics' Albert Hirshman wrote.

"Articles and books are still being produced. But as an observer and long time participant, I cannot help feeling that the old liveliness is no longer there, that new ideas are even harder to come by and that the field is not adequately reproducing itself."

The new vision of growth as epitomised by the development economists in 1970s and 1980s, was based on the premises that planning had distorting effects on economic development and deprived growth process from the benefits of market economy. Some economists who voiced criticism against conventional development economics, included P.T. Bauer, Ian Little, Anne O Krueger, Theodoer Schultz. In his book called `Dissent on Development' 1972, Bauer attacked basic premises of development thinking. Similarly Ian Little in 1982 criticised structuralist thoughts on development. Theodoer Schultz in his nobel lecture observed that a major mistake of much of new development economics has been the presumption that standard economic theory is inadequate for analysing the economic behaviour in the low income countries.

Reliance on market forces, liberalisation and reform in domestic policy was the major thrust of neoclassical resurgence. With the beginning of globalisation and economic integration among nations since 1970s, the nature of inquiry into the causes and cure of poverty of nations underwent significant change. The 1970s also witnessed growing development gap between rapidly growing economies converging towards the level of developed countries on the one hand and persistence of under development in may developing countries in Asia, Africa and Latin America on the other hand.

Chapter Four surveys the development experience of the third world and analyses conceptual and theoretical framework within which the new challenges arising from growing development gap can be met. The analysis shows that poverty alleviation and development gap continue to pose serious challenges to the theoretical framework of development economics.

The analysis in Chapter Five shows that the economic growth to be meaningful must meet the `Basic Human Needs' of the people throughout the globe. It is through the integration of development economics with welfare economics that the development economics can meet the challenge of poverty alleviation.

The fact that in most cases, overall economic growth failed of meet basic needs of poor, caused concern among the economists. Since 1970s, `Basic Human Needs' strategy had entered development debate with an emphasis on the fulfilment of social objective such as supply of clean water, education, medical facilities, housing etc. As the decade of 1980s set in, distribution and poverty issues came to the centre of the development agenda.

Chapter Five brings out poverty profile of the developing world and analyses the response of development economics to the urgent need of poverty alleviation. This chapter also surveys Indian Development Scene and brings to focus the challenge of eradication of poverty and unemployment. The analysis in this Chapter shows that poverty eradication is basically linked with the creation of employment opportunities and provision of basic needs. The analysis also shows that the theory of `Trickle down effect has not been effective to eradicate unemployment and poverty in India. The analysis brings to fore the fact that growing number of unemployed is a drain on the economy and slows the process of Indian economic development. Thus, there is a need for a development strategy to combat problem of unemployment and poverty alleviation. Towards the close of chapter V, new directions for the evolution of development economics have been identified. To meet the development challenges in 21st century, there is need to enrich the analytical and theoretical framework of development economics which will adequately address the problem of development gap and of widespread poverty in the developing world.

The East Asian Crisis of mid 1997 has added new dimensions to development debate. The crisis that engulfed several East Asian Countries including Malaysia, Thailand, Indonesia and Republic of Korea brought to focus the limitations of market economy in guaranteeing sustained rapid economic growth to the countries who had achieved in past, several decades of rapid economic growth. Intensive analysis of factors contributing to the deep recession in which the `miracle' economies were entrapped, have shown that sustained development requires appropriate institutional framework and management of macro-economic variables. The experience of the East Asian countries affected by the crisis has also shown that instability and unpredictability of financial markets can destabilise growth momentum of developing economies and therefore the degree of dependence on global finance in a developing economy needs to be carefully managed. The East Asian crisis presents new challenges for development thought and policy and opens new areas of research and study on the mechanism of mitigating risks, the globalisation presents to the efforts of developing countries to continue growth with stability.

The slide-back in the momentum of growth in East Asian economies affected by the crisis also slowed down the rapid progress that these economies had made in reducing poverty. According to some reports, the proportion of population living below the poverty line was expected to increase in Indonesia, and Thailand. In all the four East Asian Countries affected by crisis, the number of unemployed was also expected to increase. For further evolution of development thought and policy, the search of mechanism to counter the reverse trend in poverty alleviation in these economies need to be innovated. This is yet another direction towards which development economics in future should evolve.

2

Early Stages in Development Thinking: An Overview

The analysis of the causes of economic growth was one of the primary concerns of classical economists. The classical analysis of economic development began with Adam Smith's "An inquiry into the nature and causes of the wealth of Nations-1776," and was further continued in the writings of David Ricardo, Malthus, Karl Marx and J.S. Mill. The classical economists's main focus was on capital accumulation as the main factor in the creation of wealth of Nations. In course of seventy-two years from 1776 when Smith's "wealth of Nation" was published, till the publication of J.S. Mill's "Principles of Political Economy" in 1848, the growth analysis was dominated by classical economic thought. The basic concepts on which classical economic thought evolved included the principle of Laissez Faire, division of labour, free foreign trade, capital accumulation, diminishing returns and theory of over population.

ADAM SMITH

Adam Smith advocated a system of natural liberty in which each individual would be left free to pursue and advance his own interests. The system he argued will result in the greatest wealth both for the individual and for the society. This represented a fundamental break from Mercantilism. The advocates of mercantilism and government regulation had assumed that the selfish desires of individuals would lead to less wealth for all unless human actions were regulated and controlled. In Adam Smith's scheme, the pursuit of self-interest would lead to the most rapid growth of nation. Adam Smith phrased the theory of self-interest in following words:-

> "It is not from the benevolence of the butcher, the brewer, or the baker, that we expect our dinner, but from their regard to their own interest. We address ourselves, not to their humanity but to their self love and never talk to them of our own necessities but of their advantages."[1]

Unlike mercantilists, Adam Smith thought that individualism resulted in order and not in chaos. In his system, individual stands at the centre and the pursuit of self interest promotes social welfare. Smith believed that each individual while pursuing his own advantage was led by an invisible hand to promote an end which was no part of his intention. His belief in the natural order was the basis on which Adam Smith advocated the policy of Laissez Faire. Individuals left to themselves will maximise their own advantages and that will result in maximum advantages. According to Smith's natural system, the State should undertake only the duty of defence, administration of justice and the maintenance of public works which could not be maintained by individuals.

Adam Smith's investigation of causes of Wealth of nations begins right in the introduction to the volume I of the Book "An inquiry into the nature and causes of the Wealth of Nations." As to what constitutes, Wealth of Nations, he wrote:

> "The annual labour of every nation is the fund which originally supplies it with all the necessities and conveniences of life which it annually consumes and which consists always either in the immediate produce of the labourers or in what is purchased with that produce from other nations."[2]

In Smith's system, labour is the original source of wealth. The wealth from labour is however, created by the application of capital and in his thought as he explains below, capital accumulation holds the key to the creation of wealth.

"The annual produce of land and labour of any nation can be increased in its value by no other means but by increasing either the number of its productive labourers or the productive powers of these labourers; who had before been employed and labour is evidently greater at the latter than the former, that its lands are better cultivated, its manufacture more extensive. We may be assured that its capital must have increased during the interval between these two periods."[3]

While developing his theory of economic development, Adam Smith also pointed out that the productive powers of the same number of labourers cannot be increased, but in consequence of some additions and improvements to those machines and instruments which facilitate and abridge labour, or of a more proper division and distribution of employment. Thus, it is clear from the above that in Adam Smith's theory of economic development, he attached major importance to the accumulation of capital which can increase productivity of labour.

Another important determinant of economic growth according to Adam Smith is division of labour. According to Smith, once development starts, it tends to become accumulative. Given adequate market possibilities, division of labour raises the level of activity. The resultant increase in national income and the probable growth of population associated with the rise in income, not only increases the extent of the market but also produces a larger saving out of the increased income stream. Moreover, as labour becomes more specialised and markets expand, the ability and incentive to introduce `improvement of arts' increases.

These improvements still lead to further specialisation and productivity gains.

Underlining the contribution of division of labour to economic growth, Adam Smith further said:

> "This great increase of the quantity of work, which, in consequence of the division of labour, the same number of people are capable of performing, is owing to three different circumstances; first, to the increase of dexterity in every particular workman; secondly, to the moving of the time which is commonly lost in passing from the one species of work to another; and lastly, to the invention of a great number of machines which facilitate and abridge labour, and enable one man to do the work of many."[4]

In Adam Smith's theory of economic growth, the extent of the market plays a very important role. Adam Smith describes the importance of the extent of market in following words: "When the market is very small, no person can have any encouragement to dedicate himself entirely to one employment for want of the power to exchange all that surplus part of the produce of his own labour, which is over all his own consumption, for such parts of the produce of other men's labour as he has occasion for."[5]

Adam Smith made a very important point that although division of labour can increase labour's productivity in a physical sense, this division may not be profitable unless market demand is sufficiently large. This leads to the concept of external economies. In the development process Adam Smith recognises the significance of external economies. The concept of the external economies refers to a situation in which the cost curves of individual firms shift downwards because of the development of their environment. The notion of the external economies recognises the interdependence and complementarity of various sectors of the economy. As one part grows, it stimulates other parts not only by increasing demands but also by decreasing costs. For example, the growth of transportation facility in a particular area, may lead to a lowering of cost for firms using the services of the transportation industry.

The classical theory of international trade grew out of the work of Adam Smith. In a sense what Smith put forward was a theory of the interaction of trade and economic growth. In the `wealth of Nations,' great stress is laid upon division of labour as the engine of economic development. But division of labour is limited by the extent of the market. What trade does is to widen this market, which increases the scope for division of labour. Assuming that factors arc immobile internationally then trade will be on the basis of absolute advantage. The advantage of trade lies in buying commodities cheaper abroad than at home. To quote from what Adam Smith said, "it is the maxim of prudent master of family never to make at home what it will cost more than to buy all of them find it for their interest to employ their whole industry in a way in which they have some advantage over their neighbours and to purchase with a part of its produce, whatever else they have occasion for"[6]

The advantage of buying from the cheapest source was then one of the major advantages of trade; and with this was coupled with advantage of obtaining through trade, commodities which were completely unobtainable by domestic production. Trade was seen essentially as a means of disposing of surplus produce obtained by extending the division of labour beyond the scope which the domestic market could support. This is the so called "vent for surplus" doctrine of Adam Smith.

Adam Smith produced a classic case for freedom of trade. The trade increased income not only because it supported growth but it meant that commodities could be imported from where their input requirements were lowest. This in turn, minimised input requirements for any collection of goods, provided the extra output of particular kinds of goods could be disposed off through trade. Trade maximised the income which could be obtained from particular resources. Freedom of trade also ensures that capital flows to those employments where it would be most productive in increasing the division of labour. This was the message of the Wealth of Nations of Adam Smith.

While developing the rationale of free trade, Adam Smith argued against mercantilist policy of controlling trade. The advantages of free trade are explained in the following words of Adam Smith:

"To give the monopoly of the home-market to the produce of domestic industry, in any particular art or manufacture, is in some measure to direct private people in what manner they ought to employ their capitals, and must, in almost all cases, be either a useless or a hurtful regulation. If the produce of domestic can be brought there as cheap as that of foreign industry, the regulation is evidently useless. If it cannot, it must generally be hurtful. It is the maxim of every prudent master of a family, never to attempt to make at home what it will cost him more to make than to buy. The tailor does not attempt to make his own shoes, but buys them of the shoemaker. The shoemaker does not attempt to make his own clothes, but employs a tailor. The farmer attempts to make neither the one nor the other but employs those different artificers. All of them find it for their interest to employ their whole industry in a way in which they have some advantage over their neighbours, and to purchase with a part of its produce, or what is the same thing, with the price of a part of it, whatever they occasion for.

What is prudent in the conduct of every private family, can scarce by folly in that of great kingdom. If a foreign country can supply us with a commodity cheaper than we ourselves can make it, better buy it of them with some part of the produce of our own industry, employed in a way in which we have some advantage."[7]

Adam Smith went deep into the interaction between economic growth and Free Trade and explained in details the harmful effects of government control on industry. He wrote:

"If Government regulation directed the industry of a nation to produce a commodity which could be brought cheaper from abroad than it could be produced at home, the industry was turned away from a more, to a less advantageous employment, and the exchangeable value of its annual produce, instead of being increased, according to the intention of the law-giver, must necessarily be diminished by every such regulations. Then better to make his point, he took an extreme example: 'By means of glasses, hotbeds, and hotwalls, very good grapes can be raised in Scotland, and very good wine too can be made of them at about thirty times the expense for which at least equally good can be brought from foreign countries. Would it be a reasonable law to prohibit the importation of all foreign wines, merely to encourage the making of claret and burgundy in Scotland? He gave his own answer: 'If there would be a manifest absurdity in turning towards any employment, thirty times more of the capital and industry of the country, than would be necessary to purchase from foreign countries an equal quantity of the commodities wanted, there must be an absurdity, through not altogether so glaring, yet exactly of the same kind, in turning towards any such employment a thirtieth, or even a three hundredth part more of either."[8]

Adam Smith's 'Wealth of Nations' laid down the foundations of classical school of economic thought and the principles incorporated in the treatise became the cornerstone of economic analysis for over two centuries since its publication in 1776. In the history of development thought and policy, the influence of Adam Smith has been pervasive and marked. In his book, Adam Smith analysed the factors responsible for economic progress and also delineated the measures which could foster economic growth. His investigation of capital accumulation, division of labour, extent of market and International Trade have continued to provide important insights into the evolution of development theories.

The development debate which took off in postwar era still centres around the pros and cons of State intervention which Adam Smith analysed over two hundred years ago. In development thought and policy, Smith's market-system where the price mechanism operated through the 'invisible hand' of self interest has wielded considerable influence. The neoclassical resurgence which advocated market economy for economic development since 1970s, underlines the logic and validity of Adam Smith's vision of the role of market in the process of economic development. In Smith's model, market system based on the pursuit of self interest was of paramount importance. The eighties and nineties have witnessed the building up of a consensus among the development economists on the merits of market economy.

Adam Smith's advocacy of Laissez Faire and market economy has been at times seen as reflecting his disregard for social welfare. To consider Adam Smith as being devoid of human feeling is not a correct assessment. Some of his writings reflect his concern for equity in social and economic relations. In book I Chapter 8, 'Wealth of Nations', he wrote, "It is but equity besides that they who feed cloth and lodge the whole body of the people should have such a share of the produce of their own labour as to be themselves tolerably well fed, clothed and lodged." His concern for social welfare is also evident from his following words:

"Servants, Labourers, and Workmen of different kinds make up for the greater part of every greater political society. But what improves the circumstances of the greater part can never be regarded as an inconveniencing to the whole. No society can be flourishing and be happy of which the far greater part of the members are poor and miserable."[9]

While Adam Smith expounded the theory of Laissez Faire for the State, he gave selective role to the State in economic affairs which influenced the development policy in developing world, till date. While specifying the role of state in addition to defence and justice, Adam Smith said, "the third and the last duty of the sovereign of Commonwealth is that of erecting and maintaing those public institutions and whose public works which though they may be of the highest degree advantageous to a great society, are however, of such a nature, that the profit could never repay the experience to an individual or a small number of individual, and which therefore cannot be expected that any individual or a small number of individuals could erect or maintain."[10]

DAVID RICARDO

In the evolution of development thinking, the economists right from classical era, reflected on the time-dimension of the continued growth and development. David Ricardo's 'Principles of political economy and taxation' which was published in 1817 had touched on the limitations on economic growth which the system of economic forces itself generates. While Adam Smith in "The Wealth of Nations" enquired into the factors contributing to the creation of wealth, Ricardo in his "Principles", emphasised on the distributional aspects of the total produce and from his analysis, he worked on interaction of economic forces which bring stagnation and also halt growth.

While according priority to the distribution of total output among various factors of production, Ricardo wrote in "Principles of Political economy and taxation" To determine the laws which regulate this distribution, is the principal problem in political economy as much as the science has been improved by the writings of Turgot, Stewart, Adam Smith, J.B. Say, Sismondi and by others. They afford very little satisfactory information respecting the natural course of net profit and wages."[11]

Ricardo's concept of rent was the core of his system of thought. The determination of shares of other actors in the production process was related to the theoretical framework of rent accrual. Preceding the classical school, the physiocrates believed in the beneficence of nature and they had given agriculture prime importance in the creation of wealth. In Ricardo's thought, nature was niggardly and the surplus produced by agriculture is deterimental to the wealth of society. The payment of rent in Ricardo's view was unnecessary.

It is the payment of the rent to the land-lord that brings out slowing down of economy. Like Adam Smith, Ricardo also believed that growth results from capital accumulation. When profits are ploughed back into industries, the production increases and so the higher the profit which is a residual after payment of subsistence wages to labour; the higher the economic growth that an economy will register. In the early stage of a nation's growth, because of a small population only high quality of land is cultivated and farming involves low cost of production and which results in low subsistence wages. Since the profit equals, residual after payment of wages, the high rate of profit accrues to the capitalist/business class and there is no payment of rent.

In the second stage, increasing demand for labour would cause population to grow which will require an extension of the cultivated area in order to provide large amount of food. Since the less fertile land is cultivated to grow more food, because of the non-availability of more fertile land, the cost of production of food will be higher. Since the price of food will be uniform, the land owner will earn rent on the more fertile land which was being cultivated initially. The stage is thus set in when the subsistence wage is increased and the profits obtained by businessmen is reduced. In this process, economic growth finally slows down. In Ricardo's system, it is important to note that his pessimistic conclusions are determined from his theory of rent. Ricardo's concept of differential rent is explained in the following words:

"On the first settling of a country, in which there is abundance of rich and fertile land...no one would pay for the use of the land, when there was abundant quantity not yet appropriated, and, therefore, at the disposal of whosoever might choose to cultivate it.

As the population increased, however, there was an increasing demand for food, and at the higher price, additional land of lower quality could now be brought into production. This meant, however, that those who produced on land of high quality would incur a surplus, which was appropriated by the landlord in the form of rent.

It is only, then, because land is not unlimited in quantity and uniform in quality, and because....land of an inferior quality is called into cultivation, that rent is ever paid for the use of it. When land of (less) fertility is taken into cultivation rent immediately commences on that of the first quality, and the amount of that rent will depend on the difference in quality." [12]

Ricardo's concept of rent as a differential surplus unlike income produced by work had important implications and raised issues which included economic and social aspects. If rent was not a legitimate income but emerges from niggardliness of nature, higher prices for food which generated accrual of rent, was not justified. Ricardian concept thus generated conflict of interest between landlords and businessmen. The interests of the landlords were seen as antagonistic to the interests of capitalists and the cleavage stood in sharp contrast to Adam Smith's invisible hand which resulted in perfect social harmony of interests. Ricardo's analysis of rent had a profound influence on the repeal of corn laws which was subject of hot debate among policy makers in England.

Ricardo's 'Principles' also contained analysis of capital accumulation and the relationship between savings and capital accumulation. According to Ricardo, there are two ways in which capital can be accumulated: It can be saved either in consequence of increased revenue or of diminished consumption. In Ricardo's thought, whatever is saved is invested. The rate of capital accumulation is regulated by two factors: The ability to save and the will to save. The ability to save will depend on the amount of surplus or on the 'net income' of the country. Ricardo meant by net income, the amount of the surplus over total product necessary to maintain labour's subsistence level. In Ricardian system, the rate of saving is related with the rate of profit. Ricardo described the relationship between the rate of saving and profit in following words:

"Men's motive for capital accumulation will diminish with every diminution of profit and will cease altogether when profits are so low as not to afford them an adequate consumption for their trouble and the risk which they must necessarily encounter in employing their capital productively."[13]

The analysis of relationship between economic growth and International Trade in Ricardo's 'principles' can be termed as cornerstone in the evolution of development thought and policy. Ricardo highlighted the advantages of International Trade both in terms of absolute advantage and in term of comparative advantage. He explained absolute advantage of trade in the following words:

"It is quite as important to the happiness of mankind, that our enjoyments should be increased by the better distribution of labour, by each country producing those commodities for which by its situation, its climate, and its other natural or artificial advantages, it is adapted, and by their exchanging them for the commodities of other countries, as that they should be augmented by a rise in the rate of profits."[14]

Ricardo's principles of comparative advantage provided solid foundation to later theory of International Trade and as a concept has remained valid even today. Ricardo illustrated his thought on the subject in the following words:

"The quantity of wine which she (portugal) shall give in exchange for the cloth of England, is not determined by the respective quantities of labour devoted to the production of each, as it would be, if both commodities were manufactured in England, or both in Protugal.

England may be so circumstanced, that to produce the cloth may require the labour of 100 men for one year; and if she attempted to make the wine, it might require the labour of 120 men for the same time. England therefore would find it to her interest to import wine and to purchase it by the exportation of cloth.

To produce the wine in Portugal, might, require only the labour of 80 men for one year, and to produce the cloth in the same country, might require the labour of 90 men for the same time. It would therefore be advantageous for her to export wine in exchange for cloth. This exchange might even take place, notwithstanding that the commodity imported by Portugal could be produced there with less labour than in England. Though she could make the cloth with the labour of 90 men, she would import it from a country where it required the labour of 100 men to produce it, because it would be advantageous to her rather to employ her capital in the production of wine, for which she would obtain more cloth from England, than she could produce by diverting a portion of her capital from the cultivation of vines to the manufacture of cloth." [15]

Ricardo's thoughts on important economic variables such as rent, distribution and on International Trade not only influenced the theoretical framework of economists in classical era such as J.S. Mill, Malthus but also provided analytical framework for development economists. His analysis of comparative advantage as a basis for International Trade remained valid for developing countries in the promotion of exports which are necessary for financing large scale investment for industrialisation.

J.S. MILL

Modern development economics owes much to economic thoughts of J.S. Mill, whose book 'The Principles of Political Economy' published in 1848, added new dimensions to the thinking of classical school on economic growth. Mill's analysis of economic development was pathbreaking in so far it brought out non-economic determinants of development into focus. Mill's emphasis on non-economic factor is evident when he lays down conditions for the production of wealth. According to Mill, "The production of wealth is not an arbitrary thing. It has its necessary conditions; of those some are physical, depending on the properties of the matter and on the amount of knowledge of those properties possessed at the particular place and time. But other necessary conditions are related to human nature and these are the subject matter of political economy. Hence it is the object of economics to trace the secondary and derivative laws by which the production of wealth is determined, in which must lie the explanation of the diversities of riches and poverty in the present and in past and the ground of whatever increase in wealth is result for the future." [16]

Mill believed that non-economic factors played a very important role in economic affairs. Mill's emphasis on non-economic factors was also manifested from the role that he gave to education in economic development. Education in his view was necessary for bringing quality in the agents of production and for increasing technical capacity to overcome the 'niggardliness of nature.' In Mill's thoughts one can find insight into the various concepts expounded by modern development economists such as the role of human capital in the process of economic growth. Mill's distinction between economic and non-economic factors was also reflected from his theory of distribution. He distinguished beween laws of production and laws of distribution. In his 'principles', he wrote:

"The laws and conditions of the Production of Wealth partake of the character of physical truths. There is nothing optional or arbitrary in them. Whether they like it or not, their production will be limited by the amount of their previous accumulation. Whether they like it or not, a double quantity of labour, will not raise, on the same land, a double quantity of food. Whether they like it or not, the unproductive expenditure of individuals will pro tanto tend to improverish the community, and only their productive expenditure will enrich it.

With distribution it was otherwise: "It is not so with the Distribution of Wealth. That is a matter of human institution solely. The things once there, mankind, individually or collectively, can do with them as they like." [17]

Mill's concept of distribution and its relationship with social policy was remarkable in development thinking. This added social and welfare dimension to political economy.Mill shared with Ricardo the concept of 'limit on growth'. With limited land, the law of diminishing returns will prevail and the rate of growth will be adversely affected. In Mill's theoretical framework, apart from limits on growth resulting from limited land, production could also be limited by deficiency of capital. Capital depended on savings, and savings depended on profit. Link between savings and capital formation was a notable contribution to development thought at early stage in the history of evolution of development thinking.

In his concept of 'limits to growth', Mill had foreseen the counter-veiling force of technology. He saw the possibility of controlling the deminishing returns by 'additions to the general power of mankind over nature and especially by any extension of knowledge.' In this respect Mill's thought reflected great insight into the growing forces of technology which have controlled the operation of law of diminishing return in modern era.

Like Adam Smith, Mill too attached importance to 'Division of Labour' for economic development. The division of labour in Mill's view, had many advantages for production and economic development. According to Mill, division of labour increased workers's dexterity, stimulated innovation and also enabled nations to capitalise differential advantages. He also extended this concept to International exchanges and brought to focus the advantages that foreign trade gives to nation in their economic development. In his 'Principles' he stated that International Exchange enables every country to produce the things in which it has the least disadvantage. In his 'principles' Mill very clearly brought out the trade and development linkage by applying division of labour in

International Exchanges. According to Mill, trading countries produce a larger aggregagte output and enjoy larger income. Mill's theory of International Trade has influenced evolution of thought on the interaction between trade and economic growth till today.

T.R. MALTHUS

The classical economists also analysed a very important aspect of economic growth namely the relationship between economic growth and population. Thomas Robert Malthus in his book 'Essay on the Principle of Population' which was published in 1798, examined the various aspects of population growth. In his 'Essay' Malthus expressed his concern on the tendency of world population to increase more rapidly than its capacity to produce food for the growing population.

According to Malthus, population when unchecked, goes on doubling itself every twenty-five years or increases in a geometrical ratio and food production is unlikely to increase at a similar rate. On the basis of this differentiated growth rate, population will increase at the rate 1,2,4,8,16, 32, 64, 128, 256 and subsistence as 1,2,3,4,5,6,7,8,9. This difference in the growth rate of population and subsistence would result in widening gap between population and resources, required to support it. In the theoretical framework of Malthus, nature adjusts population growth to the supply of food by moral restraint, vice and misery.

Malthusian theory of population was based on the assumption that man's biological capacity to reproduce exceeds his physical capacity to increase the food supply and the ultimate check to reproductive capacity lies in limitations of food supply. The operation of 'Law of

Diminishing Returns' was integral to the Malthusian theory of population. Because of the operation of law of diminishing returns to agriculture, agricultural production will be limited and growing population will not be able to find subsistence.

The basic postulates of Malthusian theory of population could not be sustained and became invalid in view of later development. The Malthusian proposition that the only means of keeping the population within the limit of subsistence was vice and misery, was contadicted by the development of contraceptives. There were many technological developments which augmented the food supply and which made it possible to increase the means of subsistence so as to maintain a larger population at a higher standard of living. Malthus underestimated the rate of improvement in both intensive and extensive agriculture and did not assess the progress of technology.

While Malthusian theory of population could not be sustained on empirical grounds in its own time, the theory provided strong analytical support to the classical economic thought. The dependence of population growth on food supply which was a central proposition in Malthusian theory, strengthened the subsistence theory of wages which was the basis of Ricardian theory of differential rent. For developing countries, Malthusian population theory had also its relevance. For a number of developing countries, the economic development was constrained because of increasing population. The optimum theory of population even though not fully accepted by the economists, has been a part of development debate since 1950s. The fact that a number of developing countries had to adopt policies to control the growth of population, made the Malthusian theory of population relevant for the economic development of a number of developing economies in Asia, Africa and Latin America.

KARL MARX

In Marxian system of thought, the materialistic interpretation of history was the basic concept which was expounded in his book 'Das Kapital', published in 1867. Economic factors derived its importance in Marxian thought from the 'Mode of Production.' In the Marxian system, the mode of production in material life, determines the social and political relations. The mode of production under capitalism also determines class structure comprising of dominating class and oppressed class. The mode of production determines the social structure. Whenever there is a change in the mode of production and the production relations do not change, there emerges a gap which leads to social revolution.

Marxian theoretical framework's relevance for economic development was on the above interpretation of history. Within this framework, the theory of surplus value has a prominent place. There are two classes under capitalistic system viz., capitalists who own the means of production and the workers who have labour to sell. According to Marxian theory, when labour is used by capitalists in the process of production, it yields more than its own value. The value of the flow of commodities produced exceeds the value of the subsistence of the workers and the value of raw materials and equipment used in production. This surplus value is the same as capitalist's profit.

The basic marxian concept that economic development depends on 'economic surplus' is in the classical tradition of development thought of Adam Smith, Ricardo, J.S. Mill, Malthus. What differentiates marxism from the classical school is the analysis of dynamics of changes that ensues after the creation of 'surplus value'. In classical scheme, there were limits to growth which were based on 'profit'. In their system of thought, diminishing returns would set trends towards the stationary state.

In marxian system, growth under capitalism will cease because the capitalists will try to save cost by increasing the capital output ratio (per unit of labour more capital will be used) and increase in the capital labour ratio will mean that capital will increase by more than wage bill. Assuming the constant rate of exploitation, the rate of profit will fall. The crux of marxian theoretical framework is that only labour produces value and any decrease in the amount of labour in production will reduce the surplus value. The falling rate of profit further leads to unemployment and a stage sets in where increasing number of unemployed people from what he calls industrial reserve army and that starts the process of the throw of capitalism.

Marxian concept of surplus as the main locomotive of capitalistic economy influenced development thinking in the postwar era. The founders of dependency school of thought such as Paul Baran in 1957 and later, Andre Gunder Frank carried forward the concept of economic surplus in their models of economic development.

NEOCLASSICALS

From 1870 onwards, the economists shifted their attention from macro economic problems of economic development to micro economic problems related to production, exchange and distribution. Because of continued economic growth in later part of 19th century, resulting from technological progress, the pessimistic vision of the classical economists about economy reaching stationary state, no longer haunted economic thinkers. After 1870, economists known as neoclassicals attached importance to efficient allocation of resources rather than to the creation of wealth which was corner-stone of classical development thinking.

The concept of marginalism was central to the thought of neoclassical economists and hence the advent of neoclassicism in economic thought is also known as marginal revolution. There were fundamental differences between classicals and neoclassicals in the concept of the determination of value which is of vital importance for analysing economic development. The classical economists explained the value in terms of cost of production and thus determined the value of a commodity only from the supply side. On the other hand, most of the neoclassical economists explained value in term of an equilibrium between demand and supply. The demand for a commodity was determined by 'Marginal Utility' of a product and supply was determined by the cost of production. The neoclassical economists who developed the concept of 'marginal utility', included William Stanley, Javons, Carl Menger and Leon Walras.

In the utility theory of Javons, Manger and Walras, one can see the roots of welfare orientation in the economic thinking which shaped the thought of A.C. Pigou on welfare economics. Pigou's view that main motive of economic study should be to help social improvement provided important norms for the concept of "Human Face" to economic development in the modern era.

The concept of marginalism was applied to all economic sectors viz., consumption, production, exchange and distribution. A consumer is expected to distribute his given income in such a way that the marginal utility of each dollar becomes equal. Similarly in the use of factor of production by a firm, optimum profit is achieved when marginal physical product of each dollar spent in the use of factor of production is equalised. In the production sector as well, neoclassical economists probed the ways and means as to how a fixed quantity of resources could be divided into a number of competitive uses which gives equal marginal value of the resources.

Thus, what is important to note is that in the analysis of key variables such as exchange, production and distribution, the neoclassicals basically differed from the classical economists. In classical economist's thinking, the return to factors of production were determined by specific theories applied to these factors. Rent was conceived to be surplus over the marginal cost of cultivation. Similarly in classical economics, wages were determined by the long run cost of producing the means of subsistence. The determination of profit was based on the theory of residual. The neoclassical economists did not accept the theoretical framework of classical economists in the determination of returns to the factors of production. In neoclassical thought, the value of factors of production depended on the marginal productivity of these factors in the process of production. The theory of distribution and the theory of value both were based on the principle of marginalism.

ALFRED MARSHALL

Among neoclassical economists, Marshall's 'Principles' stand out as a body of thought which had profound influence on economic variables relevant for economic development. Marshall, one of the eminent neoclassicals was a great synthesiser. His theory of determination of price was a synthesis of classical concept of labour cost theory of value and the utility theory of marginalists.

The classicals such as Ricardo and Mill thought that the value of an article represent the labour cost in producing it and therefore their analysis centered on the supply as the basic determinant of value. According to Marginalists, it is the utility of a thing that determines the value. Marginalists believed in the dictum that "men dive for pearls because they are valuable; pearls are not valuable because men dive for them." Marshall considered both explanations in his theory of value which was determined both by demand and supply and applied this theory to the consumer and to the producer both. The consumer pays the price equal to the marginal utility of a product and the producer pays to the factor of production its price according to marginal productivity of capital, labour, etc. Marshall's synthesis set at rest the controversy as to what determines the price, whether utility or cost of production? Marshall's answer was both and he wrote "We might as reasonably dispute whether it is the upper or the under blade of a pair of scissors that cuts a piece of paper, as whether value is governed by utility or by cost of production."[18]

Marshall's contributions to the evolution of development thought included first a balanced concept of determination of value as outlined above and the analysis of welfare and poverty among the people. Marshall firmly believed that study of economics should enrich understanding growth-process. Marshall wrote in principle of Economics "Very little of my work, (i.e. the problem of poverty) has been devoted to any inquiry which does not bear upon how to rid of such evils in society as arise from a lack of material wealth."[19]

Adam Smith had defined economics as a study of wealth and it remained a study of wealth throughout the classical period. For Marshall, Economics had other aspects and in following words he added welfare dimensions to the study of Economics:

"Political Economy is a study of mankind in the ordinary business of life; it examines that part of individual and social action which is most closely connected with the attainment and with the use of material requisites of well being. Thus it is on the one side a study of wealth and on the other, and more important side, part of the study of the men."[20]

Marshall's writings reflected concern for the poor. He wrote "in my vacations I visited the poorest quarters of several cities and walked through one street after another, looking on the faces of the poorest people. Next, I resolved to make as thorough a study as I could of political economy"[21]

Apart from the concern of the poor and welfare of the society, Marshall also developed several concepts which later became very much relevant for development theories and policies in the third world countries. Those included idea of market-organisation, external economies, internal economies, etc. The concept of increasing and diminishing returns to scale in Marshall's thought had its implications for the fiscal policy of taxation and subsidy.

In evaluating neoclassical contribution to development thought, it is important to take into account the theory of distribution which was analysed in neoclassical economics. Unlike classical economists, the neoclassical economists related the income shares of land, labour and capital to their productive contribution at the margin and the new theory was known as the marginal productivity theory of income distribution. According to this theory, factors of production will tend to receive returns which will be determined by their marginal productivity. One of the most important premises of neoclassical economics was that a system of free markets tended to maximise individual welfare. Since consumers were assumed to try to maximise their satisfaction and since production followed consumer wants, welfare was maximised. The cost of production was pushed to the lowest through competition. The neoclassicals shifted the focus of economics from the issue of social clashes and economic conflict in interests which had been emphasised by Ricardo and Marx to theory of economic harmony.

JOSEPH A. SCHUMPETER

In the history of development thought, Joseph A. Schumpeter made remarkable contributions through his writings on the dynamics of economic development. In 1911, he developed his ideas on economic growth in his book, "The Theory of Economic Development" which was later translated in English in 1934. Schumpeter gave a new concept to development and did not believe that exogenous changes in the economy brought out development. In a static economy, what he calls 'circular flow' the development, does not take place in its true meaning. In Schumpeter's view the economy may change under pressure of circumstances such as population growth, war etc. Yet, these changes cannot be termed as development. Clarifying his ideas about these changes, he said:

"Development in our sense is a distinct phenomenon entirely foreign to what may be observed in the circular flow or in the tendency towards equilibrium. It is spontaneous and discontinuous change in the channels of the flow, disturbance of equilibrium, which forever alters and displaces the equilibrium state, previously existing. Our theory of development is nothing but a treatment of this phenomenon and the processes incident to it.

In other words, development is "that kind of change arising from within the system which so displaces its equilibrium point that the new one cannot be reached from the old one by infinitesimal steps. Add successively as many mail coaches as you please, and you will never get a railway thereby."[22]

In Schumpeter's concept, development is the result of discontinuous change and defining this, he said:

"By 'development', therefore, we shall understand only such changes in economic life as are not forced upon it from without but arise by its own initiative, from within. Should it turn out that there are no such changes arising in the economic sphere itself, and that the phenomenon that we call economic development is in practice simply founded upon the fact that the data change and that the economy continuously adapts itself to them, then we should say that there is no economic development."[23]

In Schumpeter's concept of development, technology plays a key role and economic development in his theoretical framework is synonymous with discontinuous technological change. Explaining the discontinuous technological change, he said,"In so far as the 'new-combination' (of the material forces of production) may in time grow out of the old by continuous adjustment in small steps, there is certainly change, possibly growth, but neither a new phenomenon nor development in our sense. In so far as this is not the case, and the new combinations appear discontinuously, then the phenomenon characterizing development emerges. For reasons of expository convenience, henceforth, we shall only mean the latter case when we speak of new combination of productive means. Development in our sense is then defined by the carrying out of new combinations."[24]

Schumpeter also concretised his concept by identifying the ways in which development can be generated. There are five ways in which the process of development in Schumpeterian model can be started. These are following:

1. It can arise from the introduction of a new commodity.
2. It can be the result of a new method of production.

3. It can be the consequence of the opening up of a new market.
4. It can be due to the conquest of a new source of supply of raw materials; or
5. It can emerge because of a change in the organisation of any industry.

All these cases involve a different employment of the production factors, and hence, by definition, they constitute 'development'

In Schumpeterian system, it is the function of the entrepreneur who promotes the development by introducing new combination of factors of production and what he creates is 'innovation'. Schumpeter distinguishes between capitalist and entrepreneur. Schumpeterian entrepreneur is just innovator and he is neither a manager nor he is a capitalist.

Schumpeter's theory of innovation, wielded great influence on growth analysis in 20th century. The predominance of technology in the process of production brought innovation to the centre-stage in growth analysis. International trade has assumed catalytic role in economic growth, for developing countries. For rapid and sustained economic growth, it became necessary for developing countries to gain competitive edge in international market and that by and large depends on innovation in production process.

J.M. KEYNES

In the evolution of development economics, Keynesian economics played an important role and influenced development thinking of economists who analysed the problems of economic growth. As has been seen in the previous paragraphs, the marginalists had shifted the focus of economic analysis to individual economic entities such as the consumer, the producer and the industry. The keynesian message in 'General Theory' was that the general problems of unemployment and depression in 1930s could be addressed through aggregative analysis and linkage between variables such as investment, output, savings, consumption and employment could be analysed within the macro analytical framework. The concern of development economists in analysing the growth problem of the developing world also called for macro economic analysis. This was a notable contribution of keynes towards the tool of development economics. In the 'General Theory'. Keynes provided concepts which could be used as a framework for analysing macro economic problems of unemployment. His analysis defined savings, income and investment and consumption functions within this theoretical framework. It was his theoretical innovation which later was used by economists in analysing the problems of economic development.

Keynes rejected the law of J.B. Say that any increase in output will automatically generate an equivalent increase in spending and income so that full employment will be maintained. Keynesian economics introduced changes in the basic postulate of classical and neoclassical economists that competitive forces will lead to full employment without the assistance of Government. The need for fiscal policy and for state intervention for full employment was the product of keynesian theory of employment. This greatly influenced the planned economic development in the third world in the post world war era.

Keynesian theory of effective demand had enormous influence on the contemporary economic thought. From the time of classicals through neoclassical economists, the economic problem was how to analyse the pròblem of scarcity of resources relative to unlimited human wants. This basic concept of scarcity was integral to Ricardian vision of stationary state and also of malthusian population theory. The neoclasical economists had also struggled with the problem of scarcity in dealing with the allocation of resources to optimise production. Keynesian analysis of 1930s depression brought out another dimension of economics and that was the phenomena of 'Poverty in the midst of Plenty' which had more direct relevance for the developing world. Keynes in 'General Theory' identified several factors which can cause imbalance between consumption, production, investment and employment. It was the lack of investment that resulted in low effective demand and that caused unemployment. The resources may exist but those resources may not be fully employed.

Inadequate aggregate demand causing unemployment was the key of Keynesian system of economic thought. Reliance on Laissez Faire was not the remedy for taking out the economy from the trap of unemployment and Keynesian message had these hindsights in the social philosophy of economic planning in developing countries in as much as it gives state a role in boosting spending when it was not automatic.

In the evolution of development economics, keynesian emphasis on aggregate was very significant. The neoclassicals treated all growth producing factors, such as expansion of wants, population growth, technical change as 'exogeneously' determined factors. The micro economic tools of neoclassicals could not be used for dealing with macro-economic problems which is necessary for analysing growth problems faced by developing countries.

While keynesian macro economic analysis in 'General Theory' provided analytical tools and key variables for analysing problems of economic development, it had its limitations to be used as a development theory. First, keynesian model focused on deficient demand impeding economic growth. This was valid for industrial countries where resources were not scarce and as a result supply side was not an obstacle. In the case of developing economies the underdevelopment was basically the result of lack of investible resources. Expansion of production base is necessary for economic growth in a developing economy. The second limitation of keynesian system was that it was an analysis in the short run. However, the growth is a long term phenomena and long run aspects of economic development are of crucial importance for the growth analysis.

Inspite of these limitations, some post keynesian economists built up growth models on the basis of keynesian variables contained in 'General Theory'. R.F. Harrod, a post keynesian economist, in his book 'Towards a Dynamic Economy and Domar extended the keynesian system into a long term theory of output and employment.They analysed the requirement to maintain a steady growth of full employment income. In Harrod-Domar model, capital accummulation has a double role. On the one hand, investment generates income and on other hand it increases the productive capacity of the economy by enlarging the capital stock. In brief, for steady economic growth, the volume of spending generated by investment must be sufficient to absorb the increased output from that investment. Given the margianl propensity to save, the role of increase in investment to absorb the production out of additional production capacity was brought to focus in Harrod-Domar model. The extent of the requirement of investment in Harrod-Domar model depends on the capital output ratio. Economic growth in the developing world was closely related to the increase in the investment and that reflected profound influence of Keynsian economics on modern development economics.

Keynes also influenced development policy through his emphasis on investment and risk taking. He assigned an important role to entrepreneurs in the process of capital accumulation. In General Theory, he wrote:

"If human nature felt no temptation to take a chance, no satisfaction (profit apart) in constructing a factory, a railway, a mine or a farm, there might not be much investment merely as a result of cold calculation."

Keynesian concepts of the role of a state in investment and finance greatly influenced development thinking and policy since 1950s. In General Theory he wrote:

"I expect to see the State, which is in a position to calculate the marginal efficiency of capital goods on long views and on the basis of the general social advantage, taking on every greater responsibility for directly organising investment. The state will have to exercise a guiding influences on the propensity to consume partly through its scheme of taxation, partly by fixing the rate of interest partly perhaps in other ways"

While Keynes did not write treatise on development problem as such, his essay on "The Economic Possibilities of our Grandchildren" 1931, contained analysis of long term economic progress. He laid down four conditions of economic progress: the power to control population; the determination to avoid wars and civil dissensions; the willingness to entrust to science the direction of these matters which are properly the concern of science and the rate of accumulation.

Albert Hirschman credited keynes with major methodological breakthrough which in his view made keynes not only relevant for development thinking but in fact the founder of mainstream development economics. Keynes moved away from the classical belief that the laws of

Economics are universal. Keynes distinguished between the conditions of full employment when classical postulates applied and conditions of unemployment where another set of rules applied. The concept of duoeconomics was later applied by structuralists including prebisch, Seers, Singer and Lewis in the centre-periphery model of economic development. In the realm of policy, Keyens's idea that where necessary state should intervene to stimulate economic potential, which the market will allow to go waste was later used as basis for planned economic development in many countries.

In the conditions of unemployment and underutilised capacities in the United Kingdom in 1930s, Macro-Economic Management by the State had been crucial. Keyens had given the state an important role in the maintenance of effective demand sufficient to create and maintain full employment. In case of developing countries, the macro-economic management by state became essential to create resources through investment and capital accumulation.

Keynes's economic thought also embodied basic concept of a mixed economy which was later followed by a number of developing economies. His central theme was that capitalist market economies are inherently unstable and instability results from fluctuations in the aggregate demand. The Great Depression in his view resulted from a sharp fall in investment expenditure which was occasioned by a cyclical change in the marginal efficiency of capital. The unemployment was "involuntary" and reflected a state of deficient aggregate demand. Full employment could be restored only by fiscal and monetary policy. Because of the inability of the market-forces to restore equilibrium the shortcomings of invisible hands had to be remedied by state intervention. In his famous essay "The end of Laissez-Faire" (1924) he argued that "For my part I think that capitalism wisely managed, can probably be made more efficient for attaining economic ends than any alternative yet in sight, but that in itself is in many ways objectionable. Our problem is to work out a social organisation which shall be as efficient as possible without offending our notions of satisfactory way of life"

NOTES

[1] Adam Smith : The Wealth of Nations

[2] Adam Smith : The Wealth of Nations

[3] Adam Smith : The Wealth of nations

[4] Adam Smith : The Wealth of Nations

[5] Ibid

[6] Ibid

[7] Ibid

[8] Ibid

[9] Ibid

[10] Ibid

[11] David Ricardo : Principles of Political Economy and Taxation

[12] Ibid

[13] Ibid

[14] Ibid

[15] Ibid

[16] J.S. Mill : Principles of Political Economy-Introduction

[17] J.S. Mill : Principles of Political Economy

[18] Alfred Marshall: Principles of Economics

[19] Ibid

[20] Ibid

[21] Ibid

[22] J.A. Schumpeter: Theory of Economic Development

[23] Ibid

[24] Ibid

3

Postwar Development Economists and Neoclassical Resurgence

In the postwar era, during 1950s and 1960s, the economists developed a set of theories and concepts which represented a departure from mainstream economics and which later formed foundations of development economics. We have seen in Chapter two that in the early phases of history of economic thought: the classical, the neoclassical and the keynesian, there were several ideas and concepts which had its relevance to the process of economic growth. The classical economists: Adam Smith, David Ricardo, Thomas Malthus, Karl Marx and J.S. Mill analysed the problems of long term growth. For the neoclassicals, the issue was how the market mechanism could distribute the resources among the various economic entities. Similarly, keynes's primary interest was short term problem of unemployment and depression. What the development economists in 1950s dealt with, was the problem of under development which surfaced more distinctively in view of certain historical, political and economic developments during postwar era.

There were several important developments which led to a large body of thought and a number of theories to diagnose the causes of underdevelopment and to the build-up of theoretical framework relevant for the development of poor countries. On the political front, there was the breaking up of European empire mostly in Asia and Africa who were poor and underdeveloped. The United Nations which came into being, provided important institutional framework for dealing with common problems of poverty of nations across the globe. The new nations which had emerged also wanted freedom from wants after attaining political freedom.

The other important factor contributing to the deepening of interest in the problem of underdevelopment was that the work of some economists through their economic and statistical analysis brought the gap between poor and rich to sharp focus. The publication of 'Conditions of Economic Progress' by Colin Clark and the study of national income by Simon Kuznets in the developing countries strongly influenced the economists' view-point on the problem of underdeveloped countries. The disparities in the economic growth and the persistence of widespread poverty coexisting with affluence in the industrialised world did not fit into the theories expounded by the classical, neo classical and keynesian system of thought. Technology had yielded dividends in the form of rapid industrialisation and economic growth defied the theoretical validity of stationary state of classical economists,. of capitalistic break down as predicted by Marx and of the pessimistic conclusions of Malthus and Ricardo regarding over population and law of diminishing returns. Obviously there were several theoretical gaps in the evolution of economic thought. New ideas on economic development evolved in response to the concern for poverty and the deprivation of majority of people living in third world and also in response to the lack of relevance of classical theories of economic development for the developing world.

The development economists in 1950s and 1960s did not accept theoretical framework of mainstream economics in dealing with the problems of under development. In his Essay which was published in 1963, Dudley Seers, one of the pioneers of development economics, noted that the mainstream economics was not valid for analysing the problems of developing countries. He also said that economic theory was only valid in a special case of modern industrial capitalism. In his essay, the need for a new theoretical framework for analysing development problems was clearly brought out. To quote from his essay, "Economists seem very slow in adapting themselves to the requirements of the main task of the day-the elimination of acute poverty in Africa, Asia and Latin America-just as the previous generation of economists failed to cope realistically with economic fluctuations until after the depression had brought politically catastrophic results."[1]

The concern of the economists with underdevelopment was also reflected from the statistical work which was undertaken to study the pattern of income growth in the developing countries. Colin Clark produced estimates of national income of different countries in 1940 and concluded that the world as he found was a poor place. Simon Kuznets' analysis of the income disparity among various countries further confirmed growing poverty in the world.

The evolution of development economics in 1950s was by and large, the product of a new challenge that the economists faced during postwar era which could not be addressed by classical, neoclassical and Keynesian economics. For Keynes, it was the depression that needed economic investigation and it was expanding demand and using resources was one of the basic policy prescriptions to deal with depression. The challenge of development for poor countries on the eve of their independence was how to create resources for production.

The post 1945 development economists also rejected the agenda of post 1870 mainstream economics which was concerned with the advanced industrial market economies. For development economists, the area of inquiry was how could nations that had been left behind in the growth process catch up with industrialised countries? In the development of theoretical framework which could be applicable to the specific problems of economic development, the economists differed in diagnosis as well as in cure. For some development economists, underdevelopment resulted from the lack of capital in developing countries. According to these economists, most of the developing countries were trapped in a vicious circle of low savings, resulting in low investment and low investment resulting in low income. Accelerated capital accumulation was thought to lead to the economic growth of developing economies. This concept was also based on some of the observed characteristics of the poor countries. The lack of capital in these countries was visible from the lack of investment facilities and also from very low level of productivity. The economists who belonged to this school of thought included Ragnar Nurkse, W.W. Rostow, W Arthur Lewis, Rosentein Rodan etc.

Ragnar Nurkse, in his book "Problems of Capital Formation in Under-Developed Countries-1953" and Paul N Rosenstein Rodan, in his article "Problems of Industrialisation of Eastern and South Eastern Europe" which had appeared in 'Economic Journal' June-September-43 argued that countries have to develop a wide range of industries simultaneously for sustained economic growth. The concept of 'Balanced Growth' was based on the need for the generation of demand for the product of the industries which are set up in a developing country. In the course of development, there may occur both supply and demand bottlenecks. For setting up a steel mill for example, one needs simultaneously iron and coal mines. For setting up textile mill, one needs cotton. When a textile factory produces clothes, there must be demand for the product of textile factory in the economy. The demand for textile can come from the consumer who will work in other factories, such as shoe and bicycle factory.

Other development economists such as Albert 'O' Hirschman in his book 'the Strategy of Economic Development' in 1958, advocated unbalanced growth approach. The advocates of unbalanced growth approach did not accept balanced growth approach on the ground that market for a product can be also found out through international trade. Hirschman's theory of unbalanced growth was also explained in terms of theory of forward and backward linkages in the process of industrial development. The central concept in Hirschman's theory is that of linkages. Industries with backward linkages make use of inputs from other industries. Automobile industry uses the products of machinery and metal processing plants, which then make use of steel. Forward linkages mean that industries are set up, whose products in future will be used by other industries. For example steel industry's product will be used by automobile industry.

The concept of structuralism provided one of the basic foundations on which the edifice of modern development theory was built since 1950s. The concept of structuralism can be also termed as antithesis to the basic tenets of neoclassical economic thought. According to this concept, the production structure of developing economies is basically very different from that of industrialised developed countries. Price mechanism as an equilibrating force which was the cornerstone of neoclassical economics, did not work in case of developing economies.

RAUL PREBISCH

The Structuralists did not accept the agenda of post-1870 mainstream economics which dealt with advanced industrialised market economy countries. The center - periphery thesis of Raul Prebisch and H.W. Singer and Gunnar Myrdal's thesis of 'Comulative Causation' were central to the evolution of structuralist thought. Raul Prebisch formulated his views within an international economic framework. According to his theory, inherent structure of centre-periphery relations results in unequal gains between countries in the periphery viz developing countries and countries at the centre that is industrialised countries. While diagnosing the cause of underdevelopment, Prebisch pointed out that existing trading system is based on an international division of labour which results in disadvantages for the developing countries. Under the existing international division of labour, the developing countries specialise in the production of primary products and developed countries produce industrial goods. The neoclassical theory of maximisation of gains from free trade is not valid because, for primary products sold by the countries in the periphery, the prices are low as compared to the price of manufactured goods purchased by underdeveloped countries. In other words, the developing countries suffer from unfavourable terms of trade in their trade with the industrialised countries. While developing his theory of unfavourable terms of trade, Prebisch explained that relative lower price for primary products results from inelastic demand for primary goods by industrialised countries.

Because of the operation of Engel's law which states that with increasing income, the share of income spent on food items decreases and because of the technological progress, the demand for primary products diminishes. These two factors contribute to low income elasticity demand for the product from the developing countries. On the other hand, the demand for manufactured products remains highly elastic because increasing portion of rising income is spent by developing countries on manufactured items. These factors, according to Prebisch's thesis lead to deteriorating terms of trade of developing countries. The cornerstone of Prebisch's doctrine was that economic growth of developing countries was impeded by the structural rigidities and underdevelopment was caused by cetre-periphery relationship.

To reverse this trend, Prebisch suggested rapid industrialisation for the developing economies. This will enable developing economies to attain self-reliance in the production of manufacture and will also counter the trend of falling term of trade for the product of these economies. In the postwar years, the concept of elasticity pessimism in International Trade had profound influence on contemporary development thinking. Other development economists also advocated industrialisation as the strategy for economic development. Albert Hirschman, Paul N Rosenstein Rodan advocated import substitution as a strategy for development. This was in line with Prebisch's thinking on economic development. His theoretical framework greatly contributed to formulate trade and development relationship. His thesis also laid foundation for the strategy of import substitution which was implemented by developing countries to promote industrialisation in substitution for imports. Prebisch's thought should be also evaluated against background of 1930s depression and the phenomena of unfavourable terms of trade of primary producers countries which has to some extent continued to hamper their economic growth during recent development experience. While for some countries in East Asia and in Latin America, trade propelled economic growth, for most of primary goods producing developing countries, Prebisch's concept continued to remain valid in some respect. Inward oriented policy in international trade followed by developing countries during 1950s and 1960s, was based on the strategy of industrialisation through substitution of imports by domestic production.

In Prebisch's thought, the analysis of the characteristics of 'Peripheral Capitalism' as opposed to 'central capitalism' is very important. In peripheral capitalism unlike central capitalism, the privileged consumer society is detrimental to capital-accumulation. The high social starta who imitate the consumption pattern of the center, siphon off the surplus which should have been used for capital accumulation. He also described capitalism in periphery as an imitative capitalism in which consumption pattern of central capitalism is imitated and this does not allow accumulation to fulfil its labour-absorbing function.

In analysing, how structural factors and unique characteristics of developing countries perpetuate underdevelopment in poor countries, Prebisch explained the features of 'Imitative' capitalism of developing countries. According to Perbisch, the fruits of technology are appropriated only by privileged party in the world economy. In his view, premature imitation of the consumption-patterns of the center adversely affects the process of capital accumulation in developing countries.

GUNNAR MYRDAL

Gunnar Myrdal's disequilibrium theories which he developed in 1957, formed important foundation of structuralist school of thought. In his book 'Economic Theory and underdeveloped regions' and also in 'Asian Drama', Myrdal rejected neoclassical theory of Trade which had established gains from trade to trading nations.

Myrdal explained through his concept of 'Cumulative Causation' and 'Backwash Effects' that free trade, tends to aggravate the differences between developed and developing countries instead of equalising income as was envisaged in the thesis of noted economist Samuelson. In Myrdal's opinion, the expansion of market would favour those countries which already posses developed industries because the increased import requirement will be met by industrialised countries rather than by developing countries. He emphasised that in relationship between North and South and also between advanced and backward regions in the South, favourable effects will be weak for poor countries.

In his book Myrdal explained the operation of 'Backwash Effects' in the following words:

"I refer to all relevant adverse changes, caused outside the locality as the 'backwash effects' via migration, capital movements, and trade as well as the effects of the whole gamut of other social relations exemplified above (non-economic factors)..... The higher the level of development a country has already attained the stronger the 'spread effects' will usually be. For, a higher level of development is accompanied by improved transportation and communications, higher level of education and more dynamic communication of ideas and values-all of which will tend to strengthen the forces for centrifugal spread of economic expansion or remove obstacles for its operation."[2]

In explaining the fall-out of structural patterns, Myrdal also used the concept of "cumulative causal process". According to Myrdal, changes in the economic system create conditions which perpetuate underdevelopment rather narrow the differences between developed and underdeveloped countries. The operation of 'cumulative causal process' can be seen from the tendency of investment to attract to regions/countries where already investments have been made previously. Similarly, entrepreneurs, services etc may move to already rich countries and poor regions/countries will be cumulatively improvised.

The other notable contribution that Gunnar Myrdal made to the evolution of modern development theory was his thought that equality of income wholly converged with the requirements of high economic growth. This was the central theme of his book 'Asian Drama'. Myrdal strongly advocated that income equality improves quality of life and productivity and should be considered as a productive investment for economic growth. In 'Asian Drama', he also supported institutional reforms to reduce inequality and to raise the standard of living. Myrdal also expounded the concept of 'Income-Redistribution', in his book 'The Challenge of World Poverty' and called upon international community to undertake collective responsibility for Aid to developing countries.

W.A. LEWIS

W.A. Lewis, one of the pioneers in development economics gave a theoretical framework in which saving and investment are considered to be the central force behind economic growth. In 1955, Lewis in his book "Theory of Economic Growth" wrote:

"The central problem in the theory of economic development is to understand the process by which a community which was previously saving and investing 4 or 5 percent of its national income or less, converts itself into an economy, where voluntary saving is running at about 12 to 15 percent of national income or more. This is the central problem because the central factor of economic development is rapid accumulation (including knowledge and skill with capital)".[3]

Lewis's concept of unlimited labour supply in developing countries was another vital component of his theoretical framework. The basic characteristic of underdevelopment according to Lewis is that with very large population relative to capital and natural resources in developing countries, the marginal productivity of the labour is zero or negligible or even negative and therefore development is not constrained by non-availability of labour. In Lewis's model, there is an interaction between advanced capitalistic and non-capitalistic sector which leads to increase in saving and capital accumulation which is key to economic development. Lewis also explained the mechanism how capital accumulation takes place in developing countries. In his article- 'Economic development with unlimited supplies of labour',[4] he explained that the profit will increase when wages remain at subsistence level and with increasing share of profits, the share of income and investment will also rise because it is the capitalist who saves and invests and the process does not set in the subsistence sector because of very low level of income.

While developing his theoretical framework, Lewis rejected both neoclassical and Keynesian theory as these were not applicable to developing economies. In an under-developed economy, the capitalist hires the labour from huge reservoir of disguised/unemployed labour whose marginal productivity is either zero, low or negative and since the supply of labour at low wage is elastic, the investor continues to earn profit which is used for further investment and for further economic growth.

According to A.O. Hirschman, Lewis's focus on rural underemployment was his main contribution to development theory. The existence of dual economy in a developing economy provides the mechanism through which capital is accumulated in the growth model of Lewis.

In the emergence of development economics as a separate discipline, Lewis's insight into the special problem of 'diguised unemployment' in developing economies played a very important role. Lewis rejected the validity of neoclassical economics for the solution of the problems of underdevelopment because in their scheme of thought, the economy was always at full employment and so the return of the factors of production including labour was determined by the marginal productivity of the concerned factor of production. This theory was not applicable in case of developing economies where large scale unemployment existed and the marginal productivity of labour tended to be low/zero/negative.

Lewis also did not accept Keynesian theory of augmenting effective demand to solve the problems of unemployment in developing economies. The problem in the developing economy was the lack of capital resulting from lack of savings and not lack of effective demand.

W.W. ROSTOW

W.W. Rostow in his book 'The Process of Economic Growth' developed a stage theory of economic development.[5] Rostow identified five stages of growth: the traditional society; the establishment of the pre-conditions of take-off; the take-off; the drive to maturity and the age of mass consumption. Traditional society, in Rostow's system of thought is mainly agricultural with very little savings and investment. In second stage, certain preconditions for take off are created such as expansion of basic capital in transport and communications and investment takes place upto five percent of national income.

In Rostow's stage theory of growth, the stage of take-off is very important and its analysis gives insights into the role of capital and investment in the process of economic growth. This stage is primarily characterised by increase in the rate of investment and in the technique of production. The process of 'take-off' responds to some sharp stimulus which may be in the form of a political revolution or a technology revolution or a transport-innovation. The stimulus may also come from some favourable international environment.

An essential element in Rostow's concept of 'Take Off' is increase in the rate of investment. In his theoretical framework, the proportion of net investment to national income rises from five percent to over ten percent. During 'take off' with rise in investment, industry expands and also labour grows. This also leads to transformation in basic structure of society. Then comes the stage of drive to maturity when the rate of investment increases further and averages to 10-25 percent of national income. With increase in the rate of investment, industry is further diversified and finally the stage of mass consumption is reached when in addition to production, welfare is also promoted.

In Rostow's theoretical framework, development is a linear path, through which all countries travel. The advanced countries of today had passed through these stages. The developing countries in Rostow's view, face certain obstacles and bottlenecks in moving towards "take off" and for development to take place, these bottlenecks must be removed. Rostow's theory had profound influence on the policy of International economic cooperation since 1950s and provided rationale for international capital, aid and technical assistance to developing countries. In 1968, Pearson Report, which evaluated development assistance, was to a great extent influenced by Rostow's emphasis, on the scarcity of capital, as the main missing link in economic growth which the donor country should fill up.

In its message of international cooperation and interdependence in international economic relations, Rostow's doctrine provided an alternative to the marxian and neo-marxian concept of international relations based on conflict and clash of social and economic interests. In fact, Rostow entitled his book which was published in 1960 as 'the stages of Economic Growth, a non-communist Manifesto'.

Rostow's stage theory of development was exposed to intensive debate among economists and historians. Alexander Gerschenkron, one of the noted economic historians was critical of Rostow for his defining stages only in terms of growth rates of national income. Simon Kuznets who provided historical theory of economic growth, did not agree with the division of growth process into stages. In his view, the dividing lines between stages are considerably blurred in Rostow's model.

Most of the criticisms to which Rostow's theory was subjected, centered around following two points:

1. The division of economic growth among stages, in terms of history had no empirical evidence.

2. In an interdependent global economy the late comers are not required to pass through the same stages of growth which were indispensable for industrialised countries when they started on the path of industrialisation. The developing countries can share technology from the advanced countries and can leapfrog stages of economic growth prescribed by Rostow.

In the evolution of development thinking, the birth of dependency school of thought marked very strong divergence in thinking on development. The pioneers of development economics had identified the lack of capital as the main bottleneck to development. The policy equivalent of the development theories expounded by economists from Nurkse to Rostow, was interdependence between industrialised and developing economies. This strand of thought was questioned by neo-marxist economists who founded dependency school of thought. Their diagnosis of underdevelopment was redically different from that of pioneers.

PAUL BARAN

Paul Baran was one of the founders of neo-marxist analysis of economic growth in the developing countries. In his book 'the Political Economy of Growth'-1957 he analysed the causes of underdevelopment. The Concept of 'economic surplus' was central to the development-thought of Paul Baran. In his theoretical framework, a developing country's actual surplus is different from potential economic surplus. Actual economic surplus is equal to the difference between actual current output and actual current consumption. On the other hand potential economic surplus is the difference between the output that could be produced and "essential" consumption. In Baran's diagnosis of underdevelopment, the actual surplus is much below the potential economic surplus and this results in actual rate of growth levelling at much lower rate than potential rate of growth. According to Baran, the potential economic surplus in a developing economy is drained away first by the transfer of this surplus out of country and secondly by luxurious consumption of capitalist class and by feudal lords. The economic surplus of the colonies was siphoned off by imperialist countries and that resulted in stagnation and underdevelopment in the third world.

ANDRE GUNDER FRANK

Andre Gunder Frank extended the work of Baran and added new dimensions to Baran's concept of international economic relations. In Frank's thoughts, state of underdevelopment in poor countries results from the contact with and exploitation by developed nations. While analysing the factors contributing to perpetual underdevelopment, Frank also developed the concept of metropolis-satellite relationship in which the cities extract economic surplus from the rural satellite areas and transfers this surplus to the metropolis. The perpetuation of underdevelopment in developing economies was, in Frank's view, directly the result of extraction of economic surplus from satellite countries by metropolis i.e. developed countries. For Frank, underdevelopment is the result of historical factors. In his concept, underdevelopment is not just a comparative phenomena in the sense that some places are more developed or underdeveloped than others. Development and underdevelopment both, according to Frank are related through a common historical process which they have shared for centuries. For economic development, therefore, the solution is breaking the international economic links which will remove exploitation and as a result, economic surplus will be retained at home in the developing countries.

The diagnosis of underdevelopment and its cure prescribed by the neo-marxist economist: Paul Baran and Andre Gunder Frank as analysed above, was later criticised on several grounds. Since in their theoretical framework, periphery was doomed to underdevelopment because of its links with the centre, it was necessary for developing countries to dissociate themselves from the developed countries. This logic became invalid on empirical grounds. The developing countries suffered from the lack of capital skill, technology, entrepreneurship. etc. The development experience since first development decade demonstrated the requirement of cooperation from developed countries in providing necessary capital, technology and entrepreneurship in the development-efforts of the developing countries. On empirical evidence, it was also proved that international cooperation which was based on the concept of global interdependence contributed towards generating growth momentum in developing countries. The rapid development of some developing countries in East Asia known as 'NIES', countered the dependency paradigm of isolation and delinking of developing countries from the currents of global economy.

The above survey of development thought shows that since early 1950s, upto 1970s, a number of development perspectives emerged. Development Economics became inter-disciplinary and multi-faceted The economists in the development of their concepts and paradigms absorbed the cross-current of ideas from various other disciplines such as sociology, psychology, political science etc. But yet, inspite of the multiplicity of theories and concepts, it was difficult to accept that the generalisations made by development economists could form a coherent theory of economic development.

In the introduction to 'Perspectives of Economic Development' (1970), the two development economists S.S. Campo and Hans W. Singer observed:

'A theory of economic development has not emerged at least not in the same sense that we can identify the price theory, or a pure trade theory or even a theory of growth. For development is not merely economic growth. It is a growth accompanied by structural, social and economic change. It is perhaps inevitable that the impossibility of using 'Ceteris Paribus' approach to problems of development should engender difficulties in constructing a unified theoretical framework.' [7]

The state of development economics towards the end of sixties passed through a 'Paradigm crisis'. The fundamental premises of structuralist thoughts and perspectives on development were challenged. The economists expressed concern on the inappropriateness of domestic economic policies which led to market distortions and underdevelopment. The new approach was based on the reconstruction of the 'neoclassical competitive model.' This stage in the evolution of development economics is also know as 'resurgence of neoclassicism' in development thinking. The economists who contributed to neoclassism in the persuit of economic development, included Bella Balassa, I.M.D. Little, Anne O Krueger, T.W. Schultz, P.T. Bauer etc. They laid down the foundations of new directions in development thinking. In his book 'Dissent on Development' P.T. Bauer, questioned the rationale and validity of fundamentals of theory of economic growth which was formulated by the pioneers of development Economics: W. Arthur Lewis, Gunnar Myrdal and Raul Prebisch.[8]

PETER BAUER

Bauer did not accept Lewis's emphasis on capitalist sector as a condition of economic development because this sector alone generates the required savings and investment. The disregard of agriculture as a source of savings and capital formation in a developing economy in Bauer's view could not be empirically sustained. Lewis's identification of capitalists as the only source of productive savings was also criticised on empirical grounds. In this connection Bauer cited examples of traders and peasants who also save.

Bauer also attacked Myrdal's theory of 'Circular cumulative causation' which implied that the developing countries suffer from vicious circle of poverty and that it was impossible to emerge from poverty without external aid. Bauer did not agree with the concept and stated that there are several examples of countries which have risen from poverty to riches and therefore the concept of vicious circle could not be accepted. The very existence of developed countries refuted Myrdal's thesis. Another important theme of Myrdal's development theory was ever widening economic inequality between developed and developing countries. In his book, "An International Economy," Myrdal had written "The trend is actually towards greater world inequality. It is, in fact the richer countries that are advancing while the poorer ones, with the larger populations, are stagnating, or progressing much more slowly." Bauer in his book, 'Dissent on Development' found Myrdal's observations on rising inequalities axiomatic and without evidence. It may be noted that as yet national income quantification of developing countries was not available and therefore the theory of rising inequality between developed and underdeveloped countries was not accepted by Bauer.

According to Professor Myrdal, development prospects of poor countries are prejudiced by contact with the more advanced countries because these contacts acquaint the people of poor countries with new consumer goods which raises the propensity to consume in developing countries. This results in discouraging savings which otherwise would have taken place. Bauer rejected the very logic behind this when people's material prospects are harmed if consumption opportunies are widened. Instead, according to Bauer, contacts with advanced countries promote development.

On the creation of 'Import Capacity' and consequent need for external aid, Bauer commented that large scale investment requiring large scale imports is neither necessary nor sufficient for economic development. Bauer also rejected Prebisch's concept of declining terms of trade of developing countries. He rejected this as an over-simplification and pointed out to the diversity in export mix of primary goods exported from developing countries. His study showed divergent movement of the terms of trade of exporting developing countries. P.T. Bauer was also critical of the basic concepts of economic development which were embodied in UNCTAD 1964 Conference. Referring to the background document: "Towards a need of Trade Policy for Development" known as the Prebisch Report, he attacked the concept of deterioration in terms of trade of developing countries and the paramount role that the deliberations of the UNCTAD Conference gave to capital in economic growth. In his comments, Bauer stated that "while capital accumulation is a powerful agent of material progress, it is not a necessary condition; still less a sufficient condition."[9]

The neoclassical resurgence in development thinking challenged the basic postulates of structuralist economic thought of postwar development economists. Ragnar Nurkse in 1953 and Rosenstein Rodan in 1943 had expounded the concept of 'Balanced Growth' and of 'Big Push' which called for state intervention. Planned investment according to these economists was necessary because of market failure and imperfect competition in ensuring socially optimal investment. For early development economists, such as Prebisch, Myrdal, Singer, Chenery, growth of developing countries could be accelerated through import substituting industrialisation and therefore state intervention in economic system was a policy-imperative for developing countries.

Around 1970s, the basics of postwar development thinking were challenged. There were new developments in the evolution of trade-theory which enabled the economists to analyse domestic resource cost of protection. Trade Economists such as Little (1970), Balassa (1973), Krueger (1984), showed that the incentive structure created by import substitution adversely affected the economic performance of the developing countries. This debate continued through 1980s. The economists advocated Laissez Faire and free market economies and the efficiency of state intervention were questioned by economists belonging to neoclassical school. The neoclassical resurgence in development thought was the basis on which the new perspectives on stabilisation and adjustment evolved which is known as Washington Consensus. This embodied measures which could accelerate the economic growth in the developing economies. The measures covered in

Washington Consensus included Balanced Budget, Price Reforms, stable Exchange rate, Trade Liberalisation, Liberalisation in foreign investment, Privatisation of State Enterprises, and Deregulation of markets etc. The policy of liberalisation was based on the premises that liberalisation will lead to an efficient reallocation of resources and the free play of market forces will take care of industrialisation by 'getting the prices right'. In the foreign sector it was adhering to exchange rate which reflected relative scarcity of foreign and domestic currency and in Public Sector it was the withdrawal of state from production and finance and the policy of privatisation. These shifts in policies reflected a substantial reversal of basic postulates of development economics and represented the application of neoclassicism in the solution of the problems of development. According to neoclassical school, policy variables made an important contribution to Asia Pacific dynamism in 1960s-1970s. According to economists: Little, Balassa, Krueger, economic success of East Asian NIES; who experienced the 'take-off' to sustained economic growth around the mid 1960s, was on the basis of export-oriented industrialisation.

BELA BALASSA

Bela Balassa in his book 'Policy Reforms in Developing Countries', attacked import substitution policies of the developing countries.[10] According to his analysis, while the tariffs and import restrictions contributed to the expansion of manufacturing industry in the developing economies, this was at a considerable cost to the national economies in the form of inefficiencies in the allocation of economic resources which results from distortion in product and factor prices. These policies reflected an inadequate appreciation of the sensitivity of economic agents to price signals. The direct and indirect subsidies to manufacturing industries gave rise to high profits and production with excess capacity. High profits retained in import-substitution discouraged the development of manufactured exports. Employment also suffered because strategy of industrialisation through imports-substitution hindered resource allocation according to comparative advantage. Capital goods imports were effectively subsidised through the overvaluation of exchange rates and low tariffs on the import of capital good. The employment effects of these policies were also unfavourable with repercussions on income distribution. Manufacturing sectors got high profit margin while agriculture got neglected as a result of these policies. The balance of payment effects of the strategy of import-substitution were disappointing. While these measures retarded the growth of exports, foreign exchange savings in import substitution were small. Machinery imports weighed especially heavily as under high production costs, profits could not be made with less than full capacity utilisation. In raising the cost of machinery per unit of output, the under-utilisation of capacity resulted in negative value added at market prices i.e. the foreign exchange cost of imported inputs exceeded that of domestic output. Negative world market value added is a conspicuous case of the economic cost of import-substitution. There is a cost to the national economy, whenever more domestic resources are used per dollar saved than what would have been necessary to earn a dollar through exports. In countries with high protection and distortion in factor markets, the cost showed a tendency to rise as the process of import substitution led to the production of commodities which were increasingly unsuitable to their resource endowment.

ANNE 'O' KRUEGER

An'ne O Krueger, in her book 'Perspectives on Trade and Development' brought to focus the positive impact of trade on development and linked the spectacular growth rate of South Korea, Taiwan, Hongkong, Singapore and Brazil with outward oriented trade policies.[11] The concept of optimal allocation of resources in an international economy as an important prerequisite of economic development gained ground after 1970 when the studies and researches gave sufficient evidence that higher rate of economic growth was related with outward oriented trade policy. The export oriented economies also overcome the limitations of small domestic market. Because of indivisibility, sizeable scale economies are realised by large scale production of certain items which can be possible only by export oriented policies. The import substitution policies encourage expansion of industries only upto the size of market in developing countries, and so it is difficult to make import-substitution policies economically viable alternative. Export promotion as a strategy of growth replaced import-substitution on grounds of the production functions and on ground of economies of scale. Because of difference in factor proportions needed for the industrial production, in an export oriented regime, export promotion permits rapid growth of employment of unskilled labour which is abundant in developing countries. Efficient production entails the use of a wide variety of inputs. Under a liberal trade regime, exporters have access to international markets for their inputs. Their freedom of choice permits them access to the cheapest source, thus reducing their own production cost. When industrial growth is based on the international, competition, market and firms of optimal economic size can be set up, whatever the size of the domestic market. Low cost firms can expand at the desired rate unconstrained by raw material availability or by the price inelasticity of domestic demand for the product thus leading to cost reduction. Thus, to the extent that competitive markets induce lower cost activities in the firm, an export oriented trade strategy will induce greater economic efficiency.

The development economists such as Paul Rosenstein Rodan, Albert Hirschman, Nurkse assumed that market would not adequately work for rapid development and therefore they prescribed planned economies as appropriate policy for economic development. Raul Prebisch and Hans Singer argued that world demand could not grow fast enough to accommodate rapid growth of food and raw materials on which most developing countries depended for their export. Export pessimism lent a strong support to the policy of state intervention and to adopt strategy of import-substitution. W.Arthur Lewis's theory of the labour surplus economy also provided rationale for planned economy.

Policy formulation in developing countries was largely based on these premises until the beginning of 1970s, when the trend in development policy and thought changed in response to neoclassical resurgence in development thinking. One of the factors contributing to the neoclassical resurgence in early 1970s was the failure of interventionist development strategy. Towards this direction, detailed studies by a number of development economists on the consequence of interventionist strategy for development followed by developing economies showed the deficiencies in the strategy. Anne O Krueger's article, "the Political Economy of Rent Seeking" which appeared in American Economic Review in 1974 and Henry G Brucon's article "the import-substitution strategy of Economic Development" which appeared in Pakistan Development Review in 1970 brought to focus the inefficiencies of the regulated developing economies.

By the late 1970s, a series of country-studies by trade economists, Bela Balassa, Jagdish Bhagwati and Anne Krueger established a strong empirical case for outward oriented strategy for economic development which was different from the strategy of the planned economy system. A major explanatory factor was the differences in economic policies pursued by the developing countries. The highly successful developing countries had liberalised trade and payment regimes and had relatively liberal economic policies. A market is liberalised if there are no quantitative restrictions attempting to control either buyers or sellers. The controlled markets in the developing countries include foreign exchange market, financial market, labour market, agricultural commodites market. Inflation results from these controls when the government obtains control over resources without offsetting tax increases. Similarly when direct controls on food prices are imposed and when food prices to consumers are maintained at below market level through rationing while farmers are paid at higher prices distortion in the prices occurs. In many cases, government controls the prices of public sector services inspite of inflation. Thus control results in financial losses and budget deficit and further increases the degree of distortion in the market. Foreign exchange market, credit and labour play key roles in the allocation of resources throughout the economy. When these are controlled, the cost can be high and the efficiency in the economy cannot be ensured without liberalisation. That was the message of neoclassical resurgence in early 1970s.

The development scenario in 1970s also witnessed growing divergence in economic performance of developing countries. Some of the East Asian countries emerged as a successful group of developing countries, whose growth outpaced the growth rate of the developing countries as well as of industrialised countries. On the other hand, sub Saharan Africa (SSA) and some other developing countries suffered very low rate of economic growth. The heterogeneity of the growth performance gave rise to the view that, more than any other factor, it is the development policy and economic management which is important for economic development.

The structuralist's concept that poor countries were structurally different from the advanced industrial economies and required a distinct set of policies for development was challenged. The counter-revolution in development economics (1970-80) did not accept a special/general distinction and argued for 'Mono-economics' and for an economics that was universally applicable to all countries. The poor performance of developing countries also put the structuralists on defensive and the dominant development thinking in 1980s was the revival of 'Mono-economics'.

The building up of a consensus on development policy, based on neoclassical surgence however passed through a rocky road in view of growing divergence in growth performance of the developing countries. As will be seen in Chapter IV, except for a few developing countries, the pace of development was very slow in a number of developing countries. The development debate has further intensified after mid 1997 East Asian crisis. The downturn in the momentum of growth in East Asian countries has raised fresh questions on the effectiveness of market-forces in sustaining high rate of growth in developing countries.

NOTES

1 Dudley Seers : The Limitation of the Special Ease-Bulletin of the Oxford University Institute of Statistics Vol. 28 No. 2 May 1963

2 Gunnar Myrdal: Economic Theory and Underdeveloped Regions.

3 W.A. Lewis: Theory of Economic Growth

4 W.A. Lewis: Economic Development with Unlimited Supplies of Labour Manchester School-May 1954

5 W.W. Rostow: The Process of Economic Growth: Norton, New York- 1952

6 Paul Baran: The Political Economy of Growth - 1957

[7] A.G. Frank: Capitalism and Underdevelopment in Latin America: Historical Studies of Chile and Brazil-monthly review New York 1967

[8] Paul Streeten (ed): Perspectives on Development 1970

[9] P.T. Bauer: Dissent on Development 1968

[10] Ibid

[11] Bela Balassa: Policy Reform in Developing Countries

[12] Anne O Kruguer: Perspectives on Trade and Development

4

Development Thought at Crossroads

The basic concept underlying the evolution of development thinking since 1950s was that the developing countries will grow fast enough to catch up with the industrialised economies. This optimism was based on the GERSCHENKRON's concept of 'Advantage of Backwardness' which meant that developing economies will gain from the advanced technology already available and will not have to wait like industrially advanced economies[1]. It was also expected that high marginal efficiency of capital in developing economies will yield higher rate of economic growth in comparison to the advanced economies whose marginal efficiency of capital has diminished.[2]

Since 1960 and through 1970s, economic growth was rapid in some developing countries. However, in a number of developing economies, there was a 'growth melt down'. The development experience of the developing world showed that economic catch up was a feature of a very small group of economies known as NIES.[3] For most developing countries, per capita growth rate lagged behind that of developed countries. Since 1980s, growth slowed down in much of the developing world, particularly in Latin America and Africa. Between, 1965-1995, on average, per capita income in Africa fell from 14 percent that of the industrialised countries to a mere 7 percent of the income of developed countries. In 1979, per capita GDP for developing countries in Latin America, was around 36 percent of the level of industrial countries. In 1995, their per capita income was only 25 percent of the developed countries. By contrast, the rapid growth of the East Asian Newly Industrialising Economies secured (NIES) a per capita income increase from 18 percent of the industrial countries level in 1965 to 66 percent in 1995.[4] As will be seen in the Table 4.1 according to calculation of UNCTAD sectt only a small group of newly industrialising economies sustained growth rates above the growth rates in OECD nations. For most of the developing countries, growth rates have either lagged behind or have been only marginally above (OECD). Taking real GDP growth as a bench-mark, the calculation shows widening income gap between rich and poor nations.[5]

Differential growth trends between 1960-80, resulted in the clustering of the developing countries around higher and lower growth poles. The landscape of the world economy has become polarised. According to a UNCTAD study of the 98 developing countries, 40 countries had income levels over 20 percent of the average per capita income of the G-7 countries in 1960 and 14 countries had over 40 percent of the income of G-7 countries. By 1990, the figures had fallen to 29 and 11 respectively.[6]

Not only that the developing countries failed to move closer to the developed countries, there has been a strong divergence within the developing world itself. Over the years, there has been a significant increase in the absolute income-gap between the richest and the poorest developing countries. In 1960, the richest developing economy in terms of purchasing power parity, was venezuela with a per capita income of $ 6,338 and the poorest was Lesotho, with only $ 313. By 1990, the richest was Hongkong with per capita income of $14,849 and the poorest Chad With per capita income of $ 399.

Table 4.1

Growth in the World Economy: Catching up by Developing Economies on OECD, 1960-1990

GDP Growth differential with OECD	1960-90	1960-73	1973-90
More than 3 Percent	Republic of Korea Singapore Hong Kong	Singapore Hong Kong	Hong Kong Indonesia Republic of Korea
1-3 Percent	Botswana Malaysia Thailand	Republic of Korea Taiwan Province of China Botswana Gabon Lesotho Namibia Swaziland Barbados	Botswana Cape Verde Mauritius Seychelles Bangladesh China Malaysia
0-1 Percent	Indonesia Barbados Lesotho Morocco Tunisia Seychelles	Nigeria jordan Malaysia Thailand Brazil Panama	Cameroon Lesotho Morocco Tunisia India Pakistan Syrian Arab Republic Myanmar Sarbados
Memo Item: Annual average growth of real GDP in OECD (percent)	3.2	4.4	2.2

Source: UNCTAD: Trade and Development Report 1997

According to the World Development Report of 1992, average per capita income per year in 1990 ranged from the level of around $US 20,000 in the high income countries of OECD to $ 100 in countries at the bottom of the low income group. Out of the total global population of 5.3 billion (1990), high income countries with per capita income of about $ 10,000 numbered only 800 million. Thus 15 percent of the world population receives 70 percent of the world income, on the other hand 3.1 billion people or about 60 percent of world population, in low income countries with per capita income of below $ 600 receive only 4 percent of the world income. [7]

The persistence of the wide income disparity between developed and developing countries has made the task of catching up with the developed countries difficult and the goal appears to be distant. It has also led to an intensive analysis of the development experience of the developing countries. This helped in identitying factors which contributed to widening development gap between developing and developed countries. The set back to the economic growth of the developing countries in 1980s increased the absolute income gap between the developed and developing countries by over $ 1,900 (in 1980 prices) during the first eight years of 1980s. Please see table 4.2.

In relative terms, 'per capita income in developing countries fell from 9.2 percent of that in developed market economy countries in 1980 to 7.7 percent in 1988. The rate of decline in per capita income of developing countries was markedly differentiated. In certain regions, the decline was very significant. In sub Saharan Africa during the first eight years on the 1980s, the decline amounted to about twice the income gained during proceeding ten years. In West Asia and North Africa, the income gained in 1970s was almost wiped out during 1980-88. The fall in per capita income in Latin America was substantial. In many indebted countries, especially in Latin America, declining real output growth was compounded by accelerating inflation. This pattern of declining income contrasted sharply with income growth in East Asian and South Asian countries. The 1980s, thus, firmly established unequal pattern of growth in income among developing countries. In the beginning of 1980s, the world economy went through one of the most protracted recessions. Economic growth in the developed and market economy countries came to a virtual halt during 1980-82. The volume of world trade declined and primary commodity prices dropped. The terms of trade turned sharply against primary goods exporters. As a consequence, the purchasing power of the exporters of the majority of the Primary goods exporters in Latin America and Africa declined sharply during 1980-82. The deterioration in the Terms of Trade contributed to the reduction in the pace of growth of developing countries who were exporters of primary products. Please see the table 4.3

The external shocks of the early 1980s were also reflected in the doubling of the debt of major debtor countries. For the developing counties taken together, the payments surplus of $ 26 billion in 1980 turned into a deficit of $ 84 billion in 1982. The deterioration affected all major country groups but reflected in particular the virtual disappearance of the large surplus of West Asian developing Countries. As the debt service became heavier and external financing became more scarce, imports had to be reduced. Even after recovery, the demand of primary products remained weak and as a result between 1982-84, the developing non-oil primary commodities exporters continued to suffer losses in export earnings. As per UNCTAD estimates, the developing countries under this category incurred losses in export earnings equal to $ 55 billion. The market conditions facing primary exports continued to worsen throughout

1980s. By 1987, the terms of trade of non-oil countries had reached the lowest level since the great depression.

Table 4.2

Per Capita Income in Developed Market-Economy Countries and Developing Countries, 1970-1988

Region	1980 Level	1970-1980	1980-1988
			(Increment)
DMECs	10183	2037	1904
Developing Countries	937	232	-8
of Which:			
Latin America	2245	561	-189
North Africa	1259	133	-141
Other Africa			
(Including Nigeria)	549	52	-96
(Excluding Nigeria)	394	-3	-25
West Asia	2893	712	-704
South Asia	232	24	75
East Asia	919	388	351

Source: UNCTAD Secretariat Calculations, based on national and international sources.

The Terms of Trade of oil exporters also fell below 1974 level. In 1986, the terms of trade of developing countries deteriorated by approximately 20 percent as both oil and non-oil export prices fell sharply. The losses in income due to these adverse terms of trade amounted to about $ 80 billion and this wiped out any gain in GDP growth recorded during these years. These external shocks had adverse consequence on the growth of GDP of developing countries. One of the consequences of external shocks was that real output growth rates started to diverge noticeably in 1980s. This divergence in growth performance was not only the result of increase in growth rate of traditional fast growers but also because of debt service payments, external payment deficits and terms of trade losses suffered by most of the developing countries.

Table 4.3

Selected Global Economic Indicators, 1975-1989 (Annual percentage change)

Indicator	1975-1977	1978-1979	1980-1982	1983-1986	1987-1989	1980-1989
World Trade	8.1	5.4	-0.7	4.8	6.9	4.1
Real GDP growth in DMECs	4.3	3.9	0.9	3.4	3.8	2.9
LIBOR	6.2	10.5	14.8	9.0	8.2	10.5
Primary Commodity prices	3.6	6.6	-6.1	-1.6	6.3	-3.4
			Developing Countries			
Terms of Trade						
All developing countries	1.4	2.0	10.1	-9.1	0.5	-3.6
Oil Exporters	2.5	4.7	19.5	-17.8	0.0	-6.8
Others	-3.1	-4.3	-2.4	-1.4	-0.4	-1.7
Exports						
Value	16.5	21.1	5.0	-3.9	15.0	1.3
Volume	10.0	2.4	-6.5	4.7	7.5	3.2
Imports						
Volume	9.3	2.3	9.4	-4.1	9.7	3.1

Source: UNCTAD secretariat calculations, based on national and international sources. Except for LIBOR (average annual rate)

UNCTAD: Trade and Development Report 1990

While the efforts of most of the developing countries to catch up were severely constrained in the wake of development crisis of 1980s, the income gap between Least Developed Countries and developed countries has been maximum. For these countries, there has been divergence away from the growth path rather than progress towards convergence. These countries were most adversely affected by the external schocks because of their structural characteristics.

One of the development challenges has been to narrow the development gap between the Least Developed Countries (LDCs) with a population of approximately 530 million and the developed countries as well as with other developing countries falling in low income, middle income and high performing countries on the other hand.[8] Some developing countries have made substantial progress in economic development and have achieved rapid rate of economic growth and also have gained a growing share of world export markets. These successful developing countries have been able to narrow the income gap between themselves and the industrialised countries. The integration of these successful developing countries with the global economy lends credence to the theory of convergence which has been the primary thrust of development goals.

The convergence, however, has been limited to only very few developing countries in Asia and a number of developing countries suffered divergence instead of convergence. In case of Least Developed Countries, economic growth has been very slow, and has failed to keep pace with the population growth. In all the key determinants of economic growth, these countries have lagged behind. The sluggishness in growth started since 1970s and continued through 1980s and 1990s. The LDCs growth rate have lagged behind other developing countries [9]. Please see Table 4.4

Table 4.4

Regionwise Economic Performance of LDCs in 1980-1984, Estimates for 1995 and forecast for 1996

Country Group	1980-1990	1990-1994 (Annual Average)	1995	1996
Least developed countries	2.2	2.0	3.2	3.2
of which:				
LDC Africa	1.9	0.6	2.2	2.1
LDC Asia	3.1	3.9	4.6	4.8
LDC other	0.4	-1.4	2.0	1.7
Memo Items:				
World	2.9	1.6	2.6	3.0
Developed Market Economies	2.8	1.5	2.4	2.5
Developing Countries	2.8	3.9	4.3	5.0
Central & Eastern Europe	2.1	-11.4	-2.0	2.0
China	8.8	10.8	10.0	9.0

Source: UNCTAD Secretariat calculations based on national & international Statistics.

a. Estimates
b. Forecast.
c. Haiti, Kiribati, Samoa, Solomon Islands, Tuvalu and Vanuatu
d. Excluding China
e. including the former USSR.

UNCTAD: The Least Developed Countries 1996 Report

As is evident from the Table, the economic performance of the Least Developed Countries, over the last decade and a half has been poor. Across the entire LDC group, per capita output declined at annual rate of 0.3 percent during the 1980s and 1.9 percent during 1990-93. These countries face serious development problems which include rapid population growth, heavy reliance on primary products in their exports, structural constraints and low agricultural productivity. Depressed commodity prices, adverse external shocks, debt crisis and constraints on access to foreign capital have largely impeded the growth performance of these countries.[10] The depressed commodity prices and its adverse impact on their development can be analysed from the table 4.5.

Table 4.5

Primary Commodity Prices for Developing Countries (Excluding Crude Petroleum), 1980-1995

(Percentage change, annual average)

Country Group	1980-1990	1990-1994	1995
All Primary commodites	-2.3	1.8	9
Food	-3.6	3.4	4
Agricultural non-food	-1.2	1.1	15
of which:			
Coffee	-7.5	15.2	5
Copper	2.1	-3.7	25
Copra	-6.5	16.2	4
Cotton	-0.7	-3.1	23
Fish	1.6	0.4	-11
Jute	1.2	-4.0	5
Tea	2.4	12.9	-15
Tobacco	2.3	1.2	2
Real price of all primary commodites	-5.3	2.1	3

Source: UNCTAD Secretariat calculations, based on United Nations, Monthly Bulletin of Statistics.

a. Estimates

b. Deflated by unit value index of manufactured goods exported by developed market economy countries.

UNCTAD: The Least Developed Countries 1996 Report

Globalisation epitomised by the rapid growth in International trade and capital flows and the global integration of production process and liberalisation created new opportunities for the integration of the developing world with the global economy. Since mid 1980s, several developing countries have become integrated into the world economy through expanding trade and capital flow. In their growth strategy, foreign investment and transmission of technological benefits through investment and trade has added new dynamism to their economic development. Expanding international trade and foreign investment have significantly contributed to their rapid economic growth. The LDCs however were not able to benefit from expanding international trade and investment.

Least Developed Countries (LDCs) have suffered erosion in their share of world exports, and also in Foreign Direct Investment (FDI). Please see table 4.6.

Table 4.6

LDC's Share of World Exports, Imports, Foreign Direct Investment and GDP: 1980 and 1993

(Percentages)

	1980	1993
Exports	0.7	0.4
Improts	1.1	0.7
FDI Inflows	0.9	0.4
GDP	0.6	0.4

Source: UNCTAD database. UNCTAD LDC Report 1996

Most LDCS rely on exports of primary commodities for their export earnings. As will be observed from the table 4.7 trends in the world commodity markets have not been favourable for LDCs over the last decade.[12] Primary commodites have become less important in terms of the total world exports and the share of LDCs exports in the world commodity market has also been eroded.

Table 4.7

LDCs' share of World Commodity Markets

Commodity	Share of Commodity in total LDC exports	LDCs' share of World markets	
	1993	1983	1993
Fuels	24.4	0.75	1.14
Coffee	3.5	13.90	8.00
Cotton	4.3	8.29	11.78
Fisheries Commodites	2.8	1.65	1.15
Tobacco	1.6	3.64	4.80
Tea	0.9	7.35	5.71
Jute	0.5	86.81	80.58
Copra	0.1	30.79	31.70
Wood, non-coniferous	4.2	2.82	3.21
Metals and minerals[a]	13.1	3.97	1.88
Copper	7.5[b]	10.34	8.36[b]
Hies and skins	0.3	2.34	1.05
Total	63.2	7.47	6.17[c]

Source: UNCTAD database. LDC-Report 1996

[a] Includes Iron Ore, other metalliferous ores, precious metals and stones and crude minerals.

[b] 1992

[c] Weighed average (based on commodity shares in LDC exports) excluding petroleum.

The 1990s witnessed very marked increase in the flow of private capital to the developing world. Private capital flows to the developing countries increased from an annual average of $ 19.7 billion during 1983-88 to $ 84 billion in 1990-94. The magnitude of private capital flows has overtaken that of official capital flows and aid. The distribution of private capital flows had been very uneven. There has been a tendency for capital flows to be increasingly concentrated in the richest and most dynamic economies of the world. [13] During the period 1992-94, LDC's share of global FDI inflows was marginal, amounting to only 0.4 percent. Please see table 4.8.

Table 4.8

LDCs' share of World inflows of Foreign Direct Investment, 1983-1994

(Annual Average)

	1983-1988	1989-1991	1992-1994
Inflows of FDI to LDCS (t billions)	0.3	0.9	0.8
LDCs' share of world FDI inflows (%)	0.4	0.5	0.4
LDCs' share of DCs' FDI inflows (%)	1.7	2.6	1.1

Source: UNCTAD, 1995b, table 1, pp. 391-396
The Least Developed Countries Report-1996

A variety of factors have impeded the flow of Foreign Direct Investment to Least Developed Countries. These factors include falling world demand for their primary commodity exports, a small size of domestic market, infrastrcutural difficulties. Their difficulty in attracting Foreign Direct Investment threatens to exclude these countries from a major source of technological innovation and exacerbate their technological weaknesses.

For the Least Developed Countries (LDCs) outstanding external debt continued to grow in 1990s. According to estimates based on OECD data, the total outstanding external debt stock of the 48 Least Developed Countries amounted to $ 127 billion at the end of 1993 as compared with $ 117 billion at the end of 1990s. The International Community and individual creditors have made substantial efforts to provide debt-relief to the LDCs and to other low income countries. Inspite of the relief measures taken, the external debt situation has not significantly eased for the Least Developed Countries. In most of these countries, the debt burden remains enormous in relation to their economies and debt servicing capacity. The total outstanding external debt in 1993 of the LDCs corresponded to 73 percent of the combined GDP of these countries. The majority of the LDCs carry considerably heavier debt burden. In around half of LDCs, the debt is close to GDP. Excluding Bangladesh and Myanmmar, LDCs' external debt amounted to an average 114 percent of their GDP in 1993.[14]

The economies of LDCs suffer from structural rigidities, low skill capacity and poor infrastructure. The industrial base is small and the supply structure is rigid, As a result, Least Developed Countries have been increasingly marginalised in international trade. Due to high dependence of these economies on production and export of primary commodities, trade could not play the role of engine of growth and these economies continued to stagnate.

The near stagnation of many developing economies in the 1970s and 1980s, stood in stark contrast to the rapid and sustained growth of four East Asia newly industralising countries during the same period. By inducing private firms to seek markets overseas, these countries took advantage of the large world market and exposed the manufacturing firms to the competition in international markets. It was the competitive industrial base that permitted the four East Asian Countries to sail through the economic crisis of the 1970s and 1980s. This was the empirical confirmation of the proposition of the neoclassical economics that market creates competition and stimulates growth of productivity . In market economies, the profit motive forced producers, industrial firms, service industries and workers to operate as efficiently as possible and to reduce costs and to raise productivity. Trade played a major role in sustained high rate of economic growth of East Asian Countries. Their fast expanding exports resulted in higher saving-investment ratio which is necessary for high rate of growth and their economies grew through a virtuous circle of higher demand, greater investment and increased productivity growth.[15]

The East Asian NIES had several factors which favoured export led growth based on neoclassical precepts. The East Asian economies became successful in increasing their exports of products that were growing in importance in international trade during that period. In 1990, about three quarters of their export were in goods for which the share of industrial imports had been expanding over the previous three decades. They entered expanding areas of international trade. A large proportion of exports of East Asian NIES was concentrated in fast growing dynamic products. For the East Asian countries, entering and adapting to markets in the more advanced countries was crucial for establishing competitive industries. In this respect, both the first tier and the second tier NIES performed much more successfully than most other developing countries over the past three decades. The share of first tier NIES and of second tier NIES in total OECD imports rose from 1963 to 1993 where the share of other developing regions have fallen.

The other important aspect of first tier NIES's rapid growth was the attainment of dynamic competitive advantages. The sustained rise in the export would not have been possible had these economies relied only on initial comparative advantage. Such advantages, especially those related to labour intensive industries, are unlikely to persist as wages tend to rise with economic development. That is why export expansion in the textile and clothing industries in Republic of Korea, Hong Kong, levelled off. It took off in Indonesia and Thailand. The first tier NIES industries upgraded their structure of manufacturing output towards scale and skill intensive activities. By the second half of the 1980s, the share of these activities in total manufacturing output surpassed that of labour intensive products.

Exports acted as an engine of growth for East Asian NIES. The development experience amply demonstrates the positive impact of exports on savings, investment and economic growth impact of exports on development is clearly brought out by interaction among economic variables in case of Korea. In Republic of Korea by the early 1990s, the savings ratio had risen to more than 10 times the level in the 1950s, reaching over 30 percent and closing the gap with investment. Export expanded faster than investment and contributed to increasing domestic savings. In other NIES too, savings rose much faster than investment. Expansion of export enabled increased profits to be made without the need for domestic consumption to rise so as to keep pace with the growth of production capacity. During the 1950s, Gross National Savings were less than 4 percent of GDP (Gross Domestic Product) in the Republic of Korea whereas the investment ratio was nearly three times as high as the National Savings Ratio. The foreign savings financed 2/3 rd of gross domestic investment in the Republic of Korea. Investment in Republic of Korea continued to rise since 1960s. By 1980s, investment reached the level of 30 percent of the GDP. Over the entire period of 1950-94, Domestic Savings rose much more rapidly than investment. While capital goods imports can be temporarily financed by inflows of foreign exchange from sources other than exports, it will inevitably come up against the balance of payment constaint. A sustainable growth process requires mutually reinforcing dynamic interactions among savings, exports and investment.

The evolution of investment, savings and exports in all the NIES during the past three decades corresponded closely to the pattern of sustainable growth. The most important contribution of exports to growth in a developing country is the need to overcome the balance of payment constraints. The developing countries in the initial stage of industrialisation depend on import of capital goods and technology and export finances this import. In developing countries, savings also depend on exports. In the absence of exports, industry will have to depend only on domestic demand and if output equal consumption, there is no saving. Exports also help to overcome these constraints by allowing economies of scale at the firm level that can be secured from mass production techniques as well as by providing a range of externalities at the industry level including economies of specialisation. Exports of manufactures may bring dynamic advantages such as large scale of production and external economies. The weight of manufactures in the export of East Asian countries was much greater than African and Latin American countries. Manufactured goods as a percentage of South and East Asian exporters were 44 percent in 1970 as compared to 4 percent in West Asia, 7 percent in Africa and 11 percent in Latin America. By 1988, manufactured goods comprised 76 percent of South and East Asian exports compared with 16, 16 and 34 percent in West Asia, Africa and Latin America.

The contrast between the East Asian developing economies which grew at 7 percent between 1965 and 1990 which was twice as high as OECD rate of economic growth and the Least Developed Countries which registered on average GDP growth rate of one to two per cent during this period, has put the development thought and policy at crossroads. The East Asian countries have demonstrated the capacity for rapid convergence with the developed countries whereas the structural bottlenecks have constrained the developmental goals in the case of Least Developed Countries.

As pointed out in previous paragraphs, at present stage of development, the economies of LDCs face several constraints in adopting the strategy of export led growth. These include falling demand for primary and agricultural products which account for the major share of their exports. Their exports also suffer from fluctuations in prices and terms of trade losses. As the industrial base is narrow, their capacity to compete in world market is very much limited.

In the evolution of development-thinking, the decade of 1970s and 1980s witnessed a close interaction between the development experience and development thought. As we have seen in preceding paragraphs, the neoclassical resurgence which dominated development thinking with the beginning of 1970s, was reinforced by empirical evidence. The diversity in growth performance of developing countries exposed the limitations of the policies based on development theories and models and these were subject to intensive debates. There was a major shift in the analysis of development issues. Empirical studies of growth in high growth performing economies in East Asia and in other parts of the third world got an edge under new dispensation.

The interweaving of theory and empiricism which marked the evolution of development thinking since 1970s, brought it at crossroads when it is not easy to conclude that the development economics has become rendundant following the neoclassical resurgence and to predict the demise of development economics as a separate sub-discipline of economics. The analysis in this chapter brings to sharp focus a dichtomy in the development experience of developing countries. On one side of the spectrum, we have newly industrilised countries who grew at much higher rate than developed countries and on the other side of the spectrum we have Least Developed Countries where growth has been either negative or zero.

The lesson of development experience is that the heterogeneity in growth performance of the developing countries, cannot the explained only in terms of policy variations. There are structural factors in developing economies which cannot be corrected by market-forces alone. For example for most primary products, exported by Least Developed Countries, a trend towards falling terms of trade was continued for several years. Unless there is a mechanism to regulate prices of primary products, left to market, the exports of LDCs will not have developmental impact. Similarly it has also been seen that the massive flow of investment to developing countries in wake of globalisation and global economic integration, has not helped LDCs in filling their resource gap. On the criteria of profitability, very limited flow of foreign private investment could be directed towards LDCs. Unless therefore capital is pumped into their economies through international Aid, the development prospect of these countries will remain grim. As observed earlier, the terms of trade losses of these countries also need to be compensated for their economic growth. These countries have to depend on their exports earnings to pay for their import requirements of capital goods.

The concepts expounded by the development economists since 1950s thus remain valid for analysis of economic growth of these economies and for other economies where the stage has not yet been reached for market forces to play effective role in creating conditions for 'Take-off .

The recent East Asian crisis (Mid 1997), affecting Republic of Korea, Malaysia, Thailand, and Indonesia has also demonstrated that for sustained economic growth, the policy of liberalisation and open economy has certain limitations. These economies had attained sustained economic growth of 8 to 10 percent a year for decades. They also made impressive advances in social development, infant mortality, adult illiteracy, life expectancy etc. It was very remarkable that their economic growth was achieved with very significant progress in human indicators of development.

Since mid 1997 these economies slipped into deep recession. The severity of the Asian Crisis can be measured from the rate of decline in the economic growth after mid 1997. In 1998, Malaysia registered negative growth in G.D.P, so was the case with Indonesia and Thailand. The crisis has sparked off fresh debate on the sustainability and dynamism of economic growth in open economies of East Asia and the ascendancy of principles of free market economy based on neoclassical resurgence has been put to fresh scrutiny.

NOTE

[1] Alexander Gerschenkron- Economic Backwardness in Historical Perspective 1962: Gerschenkron developed the proposition that the more backward, a country's economy, the more likely was its industrialisation to start discontinuously as a sudden great spurt proceeding at a relatively high rate of growth of manufacturing output.

[2] J.M. Keynes-General Theory: Keynes developed the concept that in industrially advanced countries, the marginal efficiency of capital will be lower. A.V. Hansen, later, built up the concept of stagnation in capitalist system resulting from lower marginal efficiency of capital.

[3] NIES: Terms stood for Newly industrilising economies and included Republic of Korea, Singapore, Hongkong, Taiwan. With the attainment of rapid of growth by other South East Asian countries such as Malaysia, Indonesia, Thailand these economies are also grouped under second tier of NIES and these countries are fast catching up with developed countries. Because of rapid economic growth and high level of industrialisation, under new categorisation by I.M.F. NIES (first tier) stands for newly industrialised countries instead of newly industrilising countries.

[4] UNCTAD: Trade and Development Report 1997

[5] UNCTAD: Trade and Development Report 1997

[6] UNCTAD: Trade and Development Report 1997

[7] UNCTAD: Trade and Development Report 1997

(In addition to Trade and Development Report of UNCTAD a number of international economic institutions including World Bank, IMF, UNDP, have focused on persistent and widening income gap between developing and developed countries. According to World Economic and Social Survey 1998, between 1991-97, the per capita income of developing countries averaged at us$ 1277 on exchange rate basis as compared with us$ 25109 for developed countries during the same period on exchange rate basis.

[8] The Least Developed Countries (LDC) have suffered the widest income gap which has persisted since the start of development-decade. According to U.N. Economic and Social Survey of 1998 the per capita income of LDCs was only dollar 261 on average during 1991-97 as compared with developed economy whose per capita income averaged at US $25109 during the same period on exchange rate basis.

[9] UNCTAD: The Least Developed Countries Report 1996

[10] Ibid

[11] Ibid

[12] Ibid

[13] Ibid

[14] UNCTAD-1993-94 LDC Report: The UNCTAD study of LDC's debt and development revealed that during 1990-93, while these countries had total debt amounted to 73% of the GDP, their real annual GDP growth had averaged at 0.8% per annum, per capita GDP growth was negative at 2% and growth in export earnings was also negative at 0.9%.

[15] The Trade and Development Report of UNCTAD in its various issues especially of 1996, 1997 & 1998 has brought out a comprehensive analysis of interaction between trade, investment and growth in East Asian NIES. The analysis of contrast between the East Asian growth performance and that of LDCs is mainly based on these reports.

5

Perspectives on Poverty in Development Thought and Policy

The analysis of poverty as an important aspect of development economics got thrust and momentum in the thoughts of postwar development economists. Rationale for income-equality for economic development was brought out very clearly in the writings of Gunnar Myrdal, one of the pioneers of development economics. Gunnar Myrdal articulated his thought of income-equality in his essay which was published in World Bank publication "Pioneers in Development".[1] In his approach to development, equalisation in favour of the low income people is a productive investment in the quality of the people and in their productivity.

Positive correlation between equality and economic growth in Myrdal's thought stood in sharp contrast to Simon Kuznet's thesis expounded in his article 'Economic Growth and Income Inequality' that early stage of growth is accompanied by growing inequality and opened this question to debate.[2] In his essay, Myrdal advocated institutional reforms to raise the living standard of poor people. His concept of higher consumption level as a condition for more rapid and stable growth influenced greatly the development thinking in 1950s and 1960s.

Myrdal's view on the equality of income represented path-breaking concept in growth-economics. In his Essay he wrote "the productivity of higher consumption levels stands for me as a major motivation for the direction of development policy in underdeveloped countries. Higher consumption levels are a condition for a more rapid and stable growth".[3] In his essay, he also differentiated anti poverty policies which could be applied to the underdeveloped countries, from those which could be applied to the industrially advanced countries. He prescribed rational institutional reforms to eradicate poverty in the developing countries because the transfer of income from the rich to the poor could not be achieved in the developing countries as it could be achieved in the developed countries through taxation and through transfer of income.

Key contribution of Myrdal to the analysis of poverty was to dispel belief that there was conflict between the goal of economic equality and growth. He argued that inequality of income will not result in savings in underdeveloped countries because in these countries there was a tendency to squander income on conspicuous consumption and investment. He also stressed that malnutrition and lack of elementary health and educational facilities bring down the productivity of poor people and therefore by raising their income their productivity will increase in the early stage of economic development, Myrdal's thoughts, thus significantly contributed towards bringing the problem of poverty-eradication to the centre-stage of development agenda of developing countries.

In the evolution of thought on poverty, T.W. Schultz, made significant contributions to the analysis and understanding of various aspects of poverty. In his nobel lecture on. 'The Economics of Being Poor', delivered in 1979 in Stockholm, Schultz said, "Most of the people in the world are poor, so if we know the economics of being poor, we would know much more of the economics that really matters". Schultz's concern with poverty was also reflected in the importance that he attached to the study of economics of agriculture'. In his writings, Schultz also stressed on the relationship between agriculture and poverty. He said, 'most of the world's poor earn their living from agriculture. So if we know the economics of agriculture, we would know much of the economics of being poor'.

Schultz's concern about poverty was basic to his thoughts on economic development. His book, 'The Economics of being poor', published in 1993 incorporated his thoughts contained in his noble lecture. He noted, "there is no integrated body of economic knowledge and no agenda of economic hypothesis to get important economic question about poverty". He also commented that economists should be faulted for not bringing poverty into the analytical realm of economics.

Schultz also brought out the criterion for identifying poor people and in this context he said that three factors are important for identifying poor people. First, where half and more of real income is required to acquire food, second where life expectancy ranges between thirty and forty years and third where they have low level of skill and knowledge which are the major components of human capital. In the evolution of development thinking. Schultz's ideas brought out radical changes in approach towards eradication of poverty in the developing countries. He expounded the view that agriculture in many low income countries has the potential economic capacity to produce enough food for the growing population and the income and welfare of the people can be improved out of increasing agricultural productivity. In this context, he said that decisive factor in meeting the welfare of people is not space, or capital, but the decisive factor is the improvement in the quality of the population. According to Schultz, the human agent is critical factor in being poor and investment in improving population quality can significantly enhance the economic prospects of poor people. Schultz believed that economics can address the problem of poverty and expressing this optimism he said "poor people in low income countries are not prisoners of an iron-clad poverty equilibrium that economics is unable to break".[6] Schultz's emphasis on improving the quality of human agents through acquisition of skills later shaped development thought on poverty eradication and influenced poverty policy in the third world.

Since 1970, the study and analysis of poverty in the developing world entered a very important phase during which several development economists worked on a conceptual framework for understanding this issue. Dr. Amartya Sen's writings on the subject which included "Development which way now-Economic Journal December 1983, Poverty and Famines; An essay on Entitlement and Deprivation (1981), Choice, Welfare and Measurement (1982)-Oxford Economic Paper (July 1983) and Commodities and Capabilities (1985) gave new insight into the analysis of the problem of poverty.

In Dr. Sen's view "Poverty is not just a matter of being relatively poorer than others but of not having some basic opportunities of material well being: the failure to have certain minimum "capabilities". The capabilities are of different kinds i.e. being free from starvation. From hunger, from under nourishment, from participating in community life etc. According to Dr. Sen, poverty is not a matter of only income but it is failure to achieve certain minimum capabilities.[7] Sen's thoughts also brought to light, deficiencies of conventional income approach for the analysis of poverty. Dr. Sen's capability-based approach to poverty contrasted with seeing poverty only in terms of low income. Poverty cannot be analysed only in terms of income deprivation but more appropriate approach will be to see whether a person has ability to pursue well being. Income deprivation is only one aspect of poverty. It is not high or low income, but whether the income is adequate enough to generate minimally acceptable capabilities. Dr. Sen clarified that to have inadequate income is not a matter having income level below an externally fixed poverty line, but to have an income below what is adequate for granting the specified levels of capabilities for the person in question. In his thought, Dr. Sen emphasised that a person must have basic capabilities to obtain the elementary physical necessities such as nourishment, clothing, shelter, etc. Because of capability failure, a poor person is deprived of amenities and facilities such as health, services, education, etc. Even though there may be sufficient income, a poor person may be deprived of these basic needs and services and so social and educational conditions become important to determine the degree of poverty in society.

According to World Development Report 1991, in terms of per capita GNP, South Africa ($2,470), Brazil ($2,540), Gabon ($ 2,960), and Oman ($ 5,220) had six times the per capita GNP of China ($ 350) and Sri Lanka ($430). But these relatively richer countries give their people significantly lower ability to survive with life expectancy varying between 53 and 66 years than what lower income countries with life expectancy of 70 years and above give to their people. Similarly, Costa Rica, which is a poorer than many upper income developing countries, has a life expectancy of 75 years. U.S.A. with a G.N.P. per head of $ 20,910 has a life expectancy of 76 years whereas Costa Rica has achieved life expectancy of 75 years with a G.N.P. per head of only $ 1,780.

The improved social and educational conditions in the above statistical comparison created higher capabilities according to Dr. Sen's thesis in China, Srilanka and Costa Rica. The empirical evidence also suggested limitation of income approach in explaining poverty. The distinction between deprivation of income and that of capability to achieve elementary functioning is relevant for public policy both for development and for removal of poverty and inequality.

The relevance of capability approach to the removal of poverty is clearly established when one compares human development indicators of Kerala and other states in India. Kerala has the highest life expectancy over 70 years compared to 57 years for India as a whole. Kerala has also higher level of literacy at 91% compared to an average of 52% for India as a whole. Even with lower income, Kerala achieved high capability levels. According to Dr. Sen's concept of poverty the explanation is the difference in public policy pursued by different states with regard to literacy, health services, medical care and food distribution. Alongwith new theoretical framework for analysing poverty, the economists also debated the link between economic growth and development especially in the context of development experience of the third world. Several studies of development experience of developing countries showed that income generation alone cannot result in poverty eradication. The empirical exercise supported the thesis of Dr. Sen that poverty is not only the result of low income but it also results from the lack of capabilities which income generation alone could not create. What is needed therefore is a new thrust on creating conditions through public policy which could increase the capabilities of the poor. In policy term it means improving the quality of life, through the fulfilment of basic needs such as education, health, care. On empirical evidence, it was clearly established that some countries improved the basic conditions and facilities for their population even though they were in the lower income group. The shift of development thinking from emphasis on economic growth to the creation of necessary conditions for removing mass deprivation was further spurred by the adoption of recommendations for basic needs strategy by the World Employment Conference of the International Labour Organisation 1976. Some of the works done by Development Economists such as H.W. Singer, Gunnar Myrdal and studies by Development Research Centre of the World Bank and Sussex Institute of Development Studies, generated intensive debates on appropriate response to the development challenges which surfaced in the course of development. The intensive debate amongst the Development Economists led to the study and analysis of poverty profile of the developing countries by the UNDP, by the World Bank and by other International Institutions. According to World Development Report of 1990 it was estimated that there were about one billion poor people in the developing world in 1985.[8] The report of the World Bank also highlighted the regionwise variations in the incidence of poverty in the developing world. According to report, South Asia with 51% of the total population below the poverty line was followed by Subsaharan Africa (47% of population below the poverty line). The other regions in East Asia, China 20% and Latin America 19% and Middle East and North America at 31% had relatively moderate incidence of poverty. The existence of such a staggering number of poor in the world brought development debate closer to the human aspects of economic growth in the developing world. These statistical exercises corroborated the fact that economic growth during four decades of development could not adequately address the problem of poverty eradication. The International community expressed serious concern on this issue in the World Social Summit at Copenhegen in 1995. The Summit adopted several resolutions on the eradication of poverty and arrived at a consensus to remove it from the third world.[9]

The consensus amongst economists and the International Institutions to give human face to development was also reflected from the emphasis that was given in the various issues of the Human Development Reports of the UNDP which brought to focus the human aspects of poverty. The Annual Human Development Reports provided analytical and statistical support to the analysis of poverty in development thoughts of economists such as T.W. Schultz, Dr. Amartya Sen, Paul Streeten, Dr. Maqbool Haq. The detailed analysis of poverty in the Human Development Reports of the UNDP brought out new dimensions of the problem which reinforced the thesis of development economists that poverty could not be thought in terms of low income alone but it had to be seen in terms of the deprivation that a poor person suffers from the limitation of his capabilities. Echoing the concern of development economists, the poverty was measured in terms of human poverty index in addition to conventional income poverty index. The analysis of poverty in terms of deprivations revealed that not only 1.3 billion people in the world survive on less than the equivalent of 1 $ per day, but also a billion people are illiterate and about a billion people lack access to safe water. Even today nearly one third of the people in the Least Developed Countries are not expected to survive beyond the age of 40 years and about 840 million people go hungry. To sum up, the staggering dimension of poverty and its manifestation in terms of human misery and deprivation quantified by the International Economic Institutions, generated fresh debates on the policies to be pursued by the developing countries. The thrust of analysis in development economics shifted towards the identification of appropriate policies which could ensure both economic growth and eradication of poverty by raising income of poor. The search for suitable anti poverty policies centered around the study of policies pursued by developing countries in Asia and in the other parts of the world, who succeeded in alleviation of poverty from their economies. Towards this direction, an empirical study of the development policies pursued by East Asian countries amply demonstrated the effectiveness of measures which could generate income among the poor. It was soon realised that what was needed was a direct attack on poverty by developing countries.

For direct attack on poverty, the development policy that creates income for those who are below poverty line, is of paramount importance. Rural population which constitutes majority of poor in the developing countries has to be the prime target of development policy. The success of some developing countries such as China and Indonesia in reducing rural poverty underlines the need for a review of development policies in other developing countries. Rural poverty in China fell from 33 percent in 1978 to 11.5 percent in 1990. Similarly in Indonesia, rural poverty declined from 33.9 percent to 14.3 percent between 1978-1990. Indonesia is yet another example where between 1970 and 1987, poverty declined by 41 percentage points.

Indonesia pursued policies which increased agricultural productivity and since poor depend on farm sector for their income, the strategy proved effective in reducing poverty. Malaysia provides another example where poverty declined through increasing agricultural productivity. Between 1973 and 1987, on average, earning of rural worker rose by almost 75 percent and during this period, poverty decreased by 23 percentage points. There was a rise in agricultural productivity in the East Asian countries: Indonesia, Malaysia and Thailand who succeeded in reducing poverty. This was through this increase in agricultural productivity that the demand for the factor of production owned by the poor that is for rural labour increased.

An important lesson of development experience of East Asian countries who succeeded in poverty-alleviation is that economic growth contributed to poverty reduction because it expanded employment opportunities for the poor.

When growth is labour-intensive and employment-generating and when human skills improve, it has positive impact on poverty-reduction. The importance of employment creation in rural sector of developing economies in poverty alleviation can be also measured from the fact that as per estimates of World Development Report, 1990, 70 percent of the poor lived in rural areas in the Phillipines, about 80 percent of the poor people lived in rural areas in India and Thailand, and in Indonesia, 90 percent of poor people lived in rural areas. In the task of poverty alleviation, therefore income generation in rural area by creating employment opportunities through employment schemes such as road building, irrigation, soil conservation, flood control projects etc. can be cost effective and also productive in so far as this will result in the development of infrastructure.

This strategy will have dual advantages for developing economies, first reduction in poverty and then development. There is a direct relationship between employment and poverty alleviation. By making use of labour, the poor is provided with opportunities to use their most abundant asset, that is labour.

In the developing countries, the problem of unemployment is much more complicated than in the developed countries. In developed countries, there are trained workers, able and willing to work but temporarily without a job. In the developing countries, livelihoods are more important than wage employment. The poor in the low income countries comprise self-employed subsistence farmers who are engaged in low productivity employment known as 'underemployment', The problem of 'disguised unemployment' where the labour has zero or negative marginal productivity, was one of the key concepts expounded in the theory of growth by W.A. Lewis in 1950s. Inspite of industrialisation in developing world, the problem of 'disguised unemployment' still persists and for poverty eradication, its solution is of prime importance. It is in understanding special characteristics of unemployment problem and prescription of appropriate policies to create employment opportunities to absorb the labour that the hope for poverty eradication in the developing countries lies.

The East Asian experience in reducing poverty shows that an interlinked and coordinated policy package will be required for the attainment of this objective in the developing countries. Malaysian development policy since 1970 very clearly brings out the fact that it is the pattern of growth, rather than growth by itself that is important for the alleviation of poverty. In 1970, about 60 percent of the Malaysian population was living below poverty line. This fell to 21 percent by 1985 and to 14 percent in 1993 and it has been projected that by 2000, only 7 percent of population will remain below poverty line. One of the salient features of Malaysian development strategy which led to spectacular success in bringing down the number of poor people was that this objective was integrated with National Development strategies and the creation of employment opportunities was one of the key elements of Malaysian strategy to fight poverty. Employment more than doubled between 1970-94 and unemployment rate significantly fell.

The third important policy issue is the provision of basic services to poor. For poverty alleviation, an important pre requisite is the need to satisfy the basic needs of human beings. The Pearson Commission Report on 'Partners in Development' recognised the importance of basic human needs strategy. In 1981, Paul Streeten;s book entitled 'First Things First' expounded the thesis that the basic objective of a development strategy should be to meet basic needs of the people which can provide minimum standard of living to the people. In 1976, the International Labour Organisation

(ILO) also adopted recommendations for a Basic Needs Strategy.

It is estimated that about a billion people are illiterate in the developing world. This results in the denial of choices and opportunities to poor people. In the basic necessities of life such as water, food, habitation, health services, the extent of deprivation has assumed serious proportions. In developing world, over a billion people lack access to safe water and about 800 million people face food scarcity. Even after four decades of development it is estimated that about 766 million people have no access to health services. It has been also estimated that approximately 500 million people still do not survive beyond 40 years of age. Regionwise, the incidence of these deprivations is maximum in South Asia and Least Developed Countries including Subsaharan Africa.

Social progress is important for reducing human poverty. Chinese development experience shows that health care improvements helped in the reduction of human poverty. In China, there was a remarkable fall in infant mortality rate. Life expectancy also increased from 52.7 years to 69.45 years. Another developing country Costa-Rica improved its profile in the elimination of human poverty. Its mortality rate for children under five fell from 112 per thousand in 1960-65 to 24 in 1980-85.

It is through the pursuit of appropriate policies and by adapting basic needs strategy as a major developmental goal, a number of developing countries have succeeded in achieving remarkable reduction in human poverty.

The concern of economists with the eradication of poverty also generated debate on the impact of human capital on poverty eradication. If poverty has to be eradicated, the earning capacity of the individual has to be augmented through educational attainment of the masses. The economists adhering to human capital school such as H. Chenery, T.W. Schultz, Adelman Morris and Paul Streeten all saw the education for the poor as a part of strategy to equalise the distribution of wealth. Chenery expounded the thesis that developing countries should increase investment in education of the poor as a part of the strategy to redirect a large share of investment towards increasing the assets of the poor. The value of human capital for development was also stressed by T.W. Schultz. In his view, the ability of human agent was vital for economic development. He strongly supported the view that the investment in improving the quality of population can significantly enhance the economic prospects and welfare of the poor people because human capital contributes to labour productivity and entrepreneurial ability.

The emphasis on contribution of human capital to economic development was also supported by the growth-experience of the East Asian Countries. Their experience demonstrated important role of human capital in the process of growth.

Human capital development as a part of development strategy to tackle the problem of poverty has a strong relationship with the problem of unemployment and this also contributed to the poverty alleviation in Malaysia, Indonesia, Korea. The study of their policies shows that these countries followed a model in which the expansion of human capabilities reinforced economic growth. They invested in the development of skill of labour and at the same time the absorptive capacity of economy increased to utilise the skilled labour. This resulted in a virtuous spiral of economic growth, human capital development and reduction in poverty.

The provision of education enables poor to participate in growth process. Increasing investment in education and skill formation enhances the earning power of the poor and prevents economy from falling into the trap of manpower crunch. The message of East Asian experience is to utilise productively the factor of production which is surplus and this will call for substantial departure from traditional strategy of development in which the problem of enlarging the pool of scarce resources was accorded emphasis.

The above presents a survey of the evolution of economist's thought on poverty. It also gives an analysis of the experience of East Asian Countries in the pursuit of policies which contributed to poverty alleviation in these countries. Through interweaving of both thought and policy, four major components for a development strategy suitable for poverty alleviation emerge. It includes following:

i). Priority to increasing agricultural productivity.

ii). Creation of employment opportunities for the poor

iii). Adoption of a Basic Needs strategy

iv). Development of Human capital.

These components give us a broad framework within which we can evaluate the prospect of poverty alleviation in India, where the problem of poverty has assumed serious proportions.

The study of Indian experience in reducing the incidence of poverty provides important inputs for economics of poverty. This also shows link between generation of employment and its positive impact on reduction in poverty. The incidence of poverty has been estimated by the Planning commission as per the methodology recommended by the Expert Group on Estimation of proportion and the number of poor. According to this estimate, the incidence of poverty expressed as a percentage of people below the poverty line has declined from 56.4 percent in 1973-74 to 37.3 percent in 1993-94 in rural areas and from 40.9 percent in 1973-74 to 32.4 percent in 1993-94 in urban areas. For the country as a whole, the percentage of people below the poverty line declined from 54.9 percent in 1973-74 to 36 percent in 1993-94.

One of the points for concern in the poverty profile of India is that even though there has been reduction in the incidence of poverty between the last two decades, the absolute number of poor people has almost remained at the same level of 1973-74. As will be seen from the following table, during 1993-94, India had almost 320 million poor people and this is one of the highest in the absolute number of people in the developing countries.

Anti-poverty programmes and policies have been integral elements of India's development-strategy. These policies are based on the recognition that only economic growth will not be effective in the eradication of poverty. Poverty can be effectively eradicated if poor starts contributing to the growth by their active involvement in the growth process. The second aspect of anti-poverty programme is that only income growth cannot improve the quality of the life of the poor and for improving their living conditions, they must have certain basic minimum services. Third, direct poverty alleviation programmes which can create more opportunities for the poor in the economic process are integral to the antipoverty strategy. A number of policy measures have been taken to improve the quality of life of the poor. It has been recognised that market mechanism cannot alone facilitate the supply of basic services to the people with low purchasing power and who are below poverty line.

Table 5.1

Number and Percentage of Population below Poverty Line

Year	Rural		Urban		Combined	
	No.of persons (Lakh)	Percentage of persons	No.of persons (Lakh)	Percentage of persons	No.of persons (Lakh)	Percentage of persons
1973-74	2613	56.4	600	49.0	3213	54.9
1977-78	2642	53.1	646	45.2	3289	51.3
1983	2520	45.7	709	40.8	3229	44.5
1987-88	2319	39.1	752	38.2	3070	38.9
1993-94	2440	37.3	763	32.4	3204	36.0

Source: Planning Commission

In Indian economy, there has been a gradual increase in the proportion of casual labour, where the wage rates received by them do not ensure an adequate level of living. At the 1993-94, level of prices, the wage levels at Rs.15/- per day in rural areas and Rs. 22/- in urban areas cannot afford a reasonable level of well being. And as the employment is casual, social security also does not exist. The question relevant for poverty alleviation is that by the year 2007 when Indian economy reaches near full employment, whether we are able to ensure an appropriate level of living to the employed.

In poverty eradication, the development of human resources plays a very important role. Wages depend on the productivity of the worker and the level of skill and education attained by the labour determines its productivity. The increase in the level of skill and education will result in increased productivity in the long run because 61 percent of the work force fall in the age group of 25 to 30 years and above. For poverty eradication, what is important in the short term is to increase the earnings of the labour engaged in agriculture. In India, agriculture absorbs 57 percent of the work force. One of the fundamental features of Indian poverty scenario is that the incidence of poverty exceeds unemployment. This is because of the incidence of underemployment on large scale where a person is not fully employed. There is invisible underemployment when an employed person even though he works throughout the year but in terms of productivity or income, he earns much less then giving a reasonable standard of living. The problem of under employment and disguised unemployment complicates and aggravates the task of poverty alleviation in India.

While it is true in Indian context that all employed do not belong to the non poor category, the level of employment is one of the determinants of the of incidence of poverty. During the decade 1983 to 1993-94, employment in India increased at close to 2 percent per annum. In this period, incidence of poverty expressed as proportion of poor in population, reduced by 9.55 percentage point. The relation between employment and poverty reinforces the perception that a strategy for reduction in poverty based on employment generation has to be accompanied by measures which contribute to sharp improvement in productivity of agricultural workers.

There is a regional perspective of employment situation in India. The national perspective on work opportunities calls for further regional analysis. There are substantial demographic, economic and social variations across the States. it is estimated that work opportunities will improve in the States of Andhra Pradesh, Gujarat, Haryana, Karnataka, Maharashtra, Tamil Nadu and West Bengal resulting in a decrease in unemployment in those States.

On the other hand, the States of Bihar, Rajasthan, Uttar Pradesh, face the prospect of increase in unemployment as labour force increases by more than the increase in work opportunities. In these States, where unemployment is likely to increase, the number of workers in Agriculture is large; 69 to 74 percent of work force. The problem of underemployment and disguised unemployment is present in greater or lesser degree in all States and the growth-process is unlikely to fully correct this phenomenon during the immediate future. An Appropriate instrument for addressing the specific issues is the Employment Assurance Scheme (EAS) which is specifically designed for the purpose and the other major programme of casual wage employment operated by the Government namely the Jawahar Rozgar Yojna (J.R.Y.) should be given greater regional focus where unemployment is likely to be endemic. At national level work opportunities are projected to increase at 2.6 percent annually during the 9th Plan period (1997-2002) and labour force at 2.5 percent which will reduce open unemployment at National level. In some states, it is estimated that increase in unemployment will continue even beyond the year 2002. These States include Bihar, Rajasthan, uttar Pradesh, Kerala and Punjab. In these States, the differential between the labour force and employment growth widens during the period 2002-2007. In these States, reorientation of the employment and anti-poverty schemes is needed. The latest national sample survey has also revealed some trends which call for creation of employment opportunities in informal sector over the period 1983 to 1993-94. The proportion of those educated to a level of secondary school or higher, among the unemployed persons increased from 47 percent to 64 percent. It also shows a mismatch between the kind of job opportunities that are needed and those that are available in the job market. The need for skilled job calls for human capital development on priority basis.

In Indian context, creation of work opportunities for the unemployed is directly related with poverty eradication. It is estimated that during 1997-2002, there will be an addition of 53 millions to labour force. Work opportunities are estimated to increase by 47 million and this will result in an increase in the incidence of open unemployment by 6 million persons. This would lead to a virtual doubling of the number of unemployed towards the end of the 9th Plan period. To reduce the incidence of unemployment, acceleration in growth of economy, with special emphasis on agriculture sector, is a pre-requisite for avoiding an increase in the incidence of unemployment.

It has been estimated that the projected work opportunities during the 9th Plan will result in an unemployment rate of 1.5 percent and in Indian conditions, it will mean substantial human cost. Even if we limit our analysis to open unemployment, leaving aside under employment and disguised unemployment, the growth of employment will have to be stepped up sharply to absorb the unemployment. It is of utmost importance that the growth target of 4.5 percent is achieved in agriculture. The growth target of other sectors will also need to be stepped up. On the acceleration of growth in other sectors, such as industry, the limitation placed by structure of demand will have to be overcome. This calls for giving priority to exports where demand may not place constraints. It has been also projected that the growth rate of the economy should be stepped up at 8 percent.

Reduction in poverty requires creation of work opportunities which can absorb unskilled workers. In India, 70 percent of the work force is either illiterate or educated below the primary level. It is therefore, important to focus on those sectors with high absorption intensity of uneducated labour force. In Indian context, it is not enough to absorb the unemployed but equally important is to raise the productivity of those who are employed and whose income increases to ensure minimum living condition to raise them above the poverty line. As most of the unemployed are in agricultural sector, it is necessary to increase agricultural productivity to raise the income of employed in rural sectors.

Poverty can be effectively eradicated when poor start contributing to growth by their active involvement in the growth process. To apply participatory approach in the eradication of poverty, a number of self-employment programmes are under operation. Under self-employment programme for rural poverty alleviation, the government had launched in 1980 the Integrated Rural Development Programme (IRDP). The Programme aims at providing self employment to the rural poor through acquisition of productive assets or appropriate skills which would generate additional income to enable them to cross the poverty line. The Target Group consists largely of small and marginal farmers, agricultural labourers and rural artisans living below poverty line. For skill development of Rural youth, the government launched a Programme of Training of Rural youth for Self Employment (TRYSEM) in 8th Plan. The aim of the Programme is to provide basic technical and entrepreneurial skills to the rural people in the age group of 18-35 years to enable them to take up income generating activities. Under Integrated Rural Development Programme there are other sub-schemes which have specific objectives and targets. These include schemes to supply tool kits to rural artisans and special scheme for the development of women and children in rural areas etc.

In addition to self employment, the government also launched several wage employment programmes for the alleviation of poverty in the rural areas. There are two major wage employment programmes namely the Jawahar Rozgar

Yojana (JRY) and the Employment Assurance Scheme (EAS) in operation. The Jawahar Rozgar Yojana was launched as a centrally sponsored scheme in 1989. The main objective of the programme is the generation of additional gainful employment for unemployed and under employed persons in the rural areas through the creation of rural economic infrastructure. This programme is targeted at people living below the poverty line.

The other important wage employment scheme in the rural area is Employment Assurance Scheme which was launched in 1983. The main objective of the EAS is to provide about 160 days of assured casual employment during the lean agricultural season at a statutory minimum wages to all persons above the age of 18 years and below 60 years who need and seek employment on economically productive and labour-intensive social and community work. The IRDP would continue to be the major self employment programme targeted towards families living below the poverty line in the rural areas. The EAS would be the major wage employment programme. The thrust of the government policy is to assure at least 100 days of employment per person per year.

In order to alleviate the conditions of urban poor, a centrally sponsored programme Nehru Rozgar Yojana (NRY) was launched at the end of the 7th Five Year Plan in 1989. Then there is also a scheme called Urban Basic Services for the Poor (UBSP). Its objectives are to attain social sector goals through provision of basic services to the poor. There exists Swarna Jyanti Shahari Rozgar Yojana (SJSRY) which seeks to provide gainful employment to the urban unemployed poor by encouraging the setting up of self employment ventures or through provisions of wage employment. With a view to create employment opportunities for poor people living in the urban area, the Urban Self Employment Programme (USEP) has been also launched. Under this Programme, the assistance will be given for setting up gainful self employment venture and vocational training will be also provided to the beneficiaries. This Programme has several components which include shelter upgradation, expansion of credit, self employment scheme.

The measures outlined above to alleviate poverty aim at increasing the income of the poor by raising their earnings. Equally important is the need to improve the living conditions of the poor by improving access of poor people to the basic facilities. The low purchasing power in the hand of the poor people limits the access for the less advantaged group of the society. Through investment in social sector, human development will be accelerated and through empowerment of the poor people, population becomes a major resource for development activities and will act as an important driving force for growth and development of the economy. The government has therefore undertaken a number of policy initiatives to provide essential commodites, facilities and services based on the need of the poor people.

The government launched provision of basic minimum services in the 5th Five Year Plan. The seven basic services include provision of safe drinking water in rural and urban areas, primary health service facilities, universalisation of primary education, Public housing for all shelterless poor families, mid-day meal programme in primary schools, provision of connectivity to all unconnected villages and habitations and streamlining of the public distribution system with focus on the poor.

Table 5.2

Basic Indicators of Human Development

Year	Life expectancy at birth+ (Years)	Literacy rate@ (percent)	Birth rate (Per thousand)	Death rate (Per thousand)	Infant Mortality rate (Per thousand)	Per Capita NNP at 1980-81 Prices(Rs)
1951	32.1	18.3	39.9	27.4	14.5	1127
1961	41.3	28.3	41.7	22.8	146	1350
1971	45.6	34.5	36.9	14.9	129	1520
1981	50.4	43.6	33.9	12.5	110	1630
1982	NA	NA	33.8	11.9	105	1693
1983	55.4	NA	33.7	11.9	105	1691
1984	NA	NA	33.9	12.6	104	1700
1985	NA	NA	32.9	11.8	97	1811
1986	NA	NA	32.6	11.1	96	1841
1987	NA	NA	32.2	10.9	95	1870
1988	57.7	NA	31.5	11.0	94	1901
1989	58.3	NA	30.6	10.3	91	2059
1990	58.7	NA	30.2	9.7	80	2157
1991	59.4	52.2	29.5	9.8	80	2222
1992$	60.8	NA	29.2	10.1	79	2175
1993@	NA	NA	28.7	9.3	74	2243
1994	NA	NA	28.7	9.3	74	2334
1995	NA	NA	28.3	9.0	74	2608@@
1996p	62.4	NA	27.4	8.9	72	2761@@

Source: Economic Survey 1997-98

NA-Not Available P-Provisional NNP-Net National Product

The recognition of the importance of the provision of basic needs in Indian development policies reflects the Indian commitment to provide human face to development. There has been improvement in human indicators since 1950s when India launched on economic development. Table 5.2 shows positive movement in basic indicators of human development in India and the progress that India has made in social sector. In the field of education, a notable indicator of progress is that the Gross Enrolment Ratio in the primary stage (Classes I-V) increased from 42.6 percent in 1950-51 to 90.5 percent in 1996-97 and in the upper primary stage (Classes VI-VIII), the enrolment has increased from 12.7 percent to 62.3 percent in 1996-97. These changes have contributed to increasing the overall literacy rate from 18.3 percent in 1951 to 52.2 percent in 1996-97. Literacy has been a priority on the national agenda. The Total Literacy Campaign (TLC) has become the principal strategy of the National Literacy Mission for the eradication of literacy throughout the country. The total literacy is targeted to be achieved by 2005 A.D. Efforts have been also made to achieve the goal of universalisation of elementary education.

In order to achieve Universalisation of Primary Education, it was estimated that during 1993-94 approximately 142 million children will have to be provided primary schooling. During Ninth Five Year Plan, this number will further go up after adding additional number of children since 1993-94. Similarly in the field of literacy the magnitude of task is gigantic. India has largest number of illiterate people in the world about a third of the world's total of around 900 million. Although literacy levels have increased from 16.67 percent to 52.21 percent since independence, unrestrained population growth has proved to be a serious impediment.

Improvement in health of the population has been one of the major thrust areas in the Indian Five Year Plans. Improvement in coverage and quality of health care and implementation of disease control programmes resulted in steep decline in the crude death rate from 25.1 in 1951 to 9.0 in 1996. Life expectancy rose from 32 years in 1947 to 61.1 years in 1991-96.

Indian experience of poverty alleviation brings out the challenges that India will face in bringing down the number of poor people below poverty line which is at present estimated at 320 million. It has been explained in preceding paragraphs that it is not only income poverty but the human poverty which causes concern to the policy makers who have to formulate appropriate policies for eradication of poverty from India. Indian development experience also demonstrates that the trickle down effect of economic growth has not been effective in wiping out poverty from this country.

There are several factors which explain very slow rate of reduction in the incidence of poverty in India. India did not achieve rapid and high rate of economic growth which was achieved by those East Asian Countries (NIES) who succeeded in virtually eradicating poverty from their economies. The second factor is that the dimension of the problem in case of India is much larger than was in the case of East Asian Countries. Thirdly while the economy grew, vast number of poor people could not participate in the process of growth because of limitations on their capabilities.

In view of the existence of large number of people below poverty line, a strategy for poverty alleviation will have to include new policy initiatives which will directly create income for the people who are below poverty line. This will be possible in Indian context when large number of unemployed and underemployed who live in rural areas are employed productively by creating jobs. This will necessitate large scale investment in rural infrastructure, agro-based industries and in rural industrialisation. As most of the unemployed and underemployed are unskilled, at first stage, to attack the problem, directly and at the core, it is essential to absorb the unskilled labour in those kinds of work where skill and high level of technique is not required.

The second related policy imperative is to intensify and launch schemes which help in the development of human resources by training and imparting the skill to the unemployed. The emphasis on the development of skill and technical know how to the unemployed manpower will contribute in synchronising supply of labour with demand. The increasing investment in human capital through education and technical training was key to the development strategy of the East Asian newly industrialised countries who succeeded in rapid poverty reduction. In Indian context, poverty reduction will have to be based on the increasing absorptive capacity of the domestic economy. The creation of the employment opportunities for poor people in East Asian Economies was augmented by export sector. As is well known, trade played a crucial role in creating employment in NIES. The rapid downturn in Indian exports during last three years underlines the need for more reliance on domestic source for the creation of employment opportunities in Indian economy.

For the eradication of poverty which is a national policy commitment and which has been supported by global consensus, it is but indispensable that India gives more weight to labour intensive industrialisation in certain sectors which can absorb unemployed labour rapidly and at the same time there is no burden on public exchequer. To ensure suitable fiscal policy of providing incentive and subsidies to the enterprises which has large potential of absorbing manpower should be given priority. Policy orientation for removal of poverty must take into account the growth propelling and growth inducing effects of poverty reduction. The utilisation of idle manpower capacity results in earning of an asset which has zero productivity when not utilised. The employed manpower also adds to the reservoir of effective demand for consumption goods produced in other sectors and thus keeps the economy growing. It is the creation of demand from domestic sources that has kept India immune from disequalibriating effects of downturn in exports. Increasing employment for idle manpower will also act as an effective deterrent to the recessionary trends in Indian Economy. Even if there may not be direct and visible profitability at high rate, in labour intensive investments for employment creation, the indirect and long term gains are sufficient to take these policy initiatives.

In Indian context, the conflict between higher productivity through capital intensive investments and relatively lower productivity from labour intesnvie investments which utilise low skilled/unskilled labour has to be seen from the point of gain in social productivity. In other words, by utilising idle manpower who has no income and who are below poverty line, there is gain in terms of social productivity which will counterbalance the loss in terms of market rate of return. This is the economics of poverty which should guide the investment criteria in Indian economy. In policy terms, suitable development strategy for economic growth in India which can meet the requirements of eradication of poverty will have an amalgam of different production and investment combinations. In some part of the economy, sophisticated and capital-intensive technique will be applicable which will meet the requirements of production with high degree of technology and capital intensity. This will meet the requirements of globalisation and integration of India with global economy. Simultaneously with this sector, their will be sectors where more labour intensive techniques to generate employment will be developed. This will strengthen our domestic economic base by enlarging income of the poor and thus creating more effective demand to sustain increasing production in a growing economy.

The task of poverty alleviation in India is colossal According to an estimate of the World Bank, in 1997, 340 million people were living in poverty as compared with estimated 300 million people in late 1980s. According to our estimate 93-94 there were about 320 million people living below poverty line. In past, India has registered comparatively slow progress in poverty reduction. It will be observed from table below, that between 1975-95, India registered annual reduction in poverty at the rate of 0.9% per annum as compared with Chinese rate of annual reduction at 1.9% and Indonesian rate of reduction at 2.6%.

Table 5.3

Poverty incidence and growth rates in India and Selected Asian Countries (In percent)

Country	Poverty ratio 1975	Poverty ratio 1995	Annual Reduction 1975-95	Average GDP growth 1970-1980	Average GDP Growth 1980-1995
India	54.9	36.0	0.9	3.2	5.6
China	59.5	22.2	1.9	5.0	11.1
Indonesia	64.3	11.4	2.6	7.8	6.6
Korea	23.0	5.0	0.9	9.0	8.7
Malaysia	17.4	4.3	0.7	7.8	6.4
Philippines	35.7	25.5	0.5	6.2	1.4
Thailand	8.1	0.9	0.4	7.2	7.9

Source: Economic Survey 1998-99

It may also be noted from the table 5.3 that as compared with other Asian countries included in the table, India has to achieve much higher rate of poverty reduction to eradicate poverty because of high incidence of poverty. Indian strategy of poverty reduction has also to take into account the elimination of human poverty by meeting "Basic Needs" of the people. As has been pointed in this chapter, there has been some progress in this direction. However

Indian comparative performance in reducing human poverty is much behind the progress made by some developing countries whose achievement in reduction of human poverty has been spectacular. The gap between Indian performance and the performance of some selected countries can be seen from the table 5.4.

Table 5.4

Indicators of Human Development for Some Asian Countries

Country	Life Expectancy at birth (Years) 1995	Infant Mortality Rate (Per thousand births) 1996	Adult Literacy rate percent) 1995
India	62.4	72	52
China	69.2	38	82
Indonesia	64.0	47	84
Korea, Republic	71.7	6	98
Malaysia	71.4	11	84
Philippines	67.4	32	95
Thailand	69.5	31	94

Source: Economic Survey 1998-99

Original source: UNDP- H.D.R. 1998

The analysis of Indian performance in reducing the incidence of income and human poverty on the basis of table 5.3 and 5.4 shows that comparatively, rate of reduction has been slow.[10] The East Asian experience in poverty alleviation, both in the sphere of income and human poverty indicates that a high and sustained rate of economic growth over a period of time, has a strong positive influence on bringing down the incidence of poverty. The pattern of their development also underlines the priority of employment creation and human development in their development strategy.

In the Ninth Five Year Plan (1997-2002) India has made projections for alleviation of poverty. On the basis of 7.4 percent economic growth per annum over the course of next 15 years, private consumption is likely to grow at 7% per annum in real terms. With a growth rate of population averaging 1.54 percent per annum during this period, the per capita private consumption is likely to grow at an average annual rate of 5.5 percent. In other words, per capita private consumption in India after fifteen years may be over 2.2 times the level i.e. likely to be achieved in the base year of the 9th plan. With such substantial increase in per capita private consumption, the incidence of poverty in the country can be reduced significantly.

The case study of Indian experience of poverty alleviation completes our survey of development thought and policy which began in chapter two. From Adam Smith's search of the causes of creation of wealth to the concern of development economists to wipe out poverty from the developing world, various streams of thoughts have emerged. Economics is a social science and deals with society and hence inevitably it has to change. The basic ideas survive these changes and adapt to the changing global developments in political, social and technological spheres. The development economics which diagnosed the all pervading phenomena of underdevelopment in post world war era, survived various current and cross-currents of changing theories and policies.

Our analysis in chapter four and in chapter five, brings to focus the theoretical support that the development economics has to provide to developing countries, in overcoming their structural bottlenecks and poverty. The neoclassical resurgence and shift to market economy in development thinking does not negate the validity of the basic tenets of development economics. These innovations in development thought supplement and enrich the development economics which was founded by pioneers in 1950s.

The international economic relations have undergone profound changes, basically propelled by technological advances. The wave of liberalisation in trade, finance and investment in international economy and privatisation and deregulation in national economy, have unleashed forces towards global economic integration. This is a positive development which has contributed to accelerating economic growth in some developing countries and by increasing the flow of trade and investment has reduced the constraints on economic development. The globalisation has however left many developing countries behind, in the process of economic growth and for development economics, this dichotomy in development presents a major challenge. Through further development in its analytical framework, development economics has to identify the factors that impede the spread of benefits of globalisation, to developing countries where poverty and underdevelopment exists.

Towards this end, development economics has to evolve in following directions:

i). The diagnosis of obstacles to development among Least Developed Countries (LDC), call for extensive and intensive research in the, pattern and prospects of trade, finance, agriculture, industry and technology and human resource development.

ii) The development economics has to analyse how the forces of globalisation can positively impact the development prospects of LDC's.

iii) To study and identify the external factors which adversely affect growth process of these economies. This will include study of their sluggish export earnings, the resource gap, resulting from lack of domestic savings and from the lack of foreign investment.

iv) The advance in technology has generated forces of globalisation and through increasing interdependence a number of developing countries have reaped benefits from technological cooperation from the developed countries. in this respect, the Least Developed Countries have by and large remained insulated from the benefits and it has led to further widening of development gap. To counter this trend, a study of appropriate technology for application in those economies will be required.

v) The poverty profile of the developing world shows concentration of poverty in South Asia and Sub-Saharan Africa. There has been a rethinking on development and a consensus among development economists has evolved that through appropriate development strategy based on the fulfilment of basic needs and by creation of basic facilities, the incidence of human poverty can be minimised even in those economies where per capita income is low and the rate of economic growth is also slow.

The differentiation between income and human poverty is a great conceptual advance in development thinking which calls for the development of analytical tools to enable developing countries to give shape to this concept in their development strategy. The prospect and mechanism of the eradication of human poverty in developing countries, thus presents a new and important area of research for further evolution of development economics.

vi) In chapter five creation of employment as a catalytic agent for reduction of poverty has been brought to focus. To boost investment in projects for the creation of employment and for removal of poverty has to be treated as an input in the creation of national wealth and income. In its further theoretical evolution, development economics has to provide new analytical tools to establish interaction between reduction in poverty and its positive impact on economic growth.

This conceptual advance in the development thinking will provide a theoretical support to developing countries in allocating an increasing proportion of the investible resources for poverty alleviation programmes.

NOTES

Gunnar Myrdal" Essay entitled 'International Inequality and Foreign Aid in Retrospect' Published in Pioneers in Development

2 Simon Kuznets: 'Economic Growth and Income Inequality'- American Economic Review Vol. 45 No.1-March 1955

3 Gunnar Myrdal: Essay entitled 'International Inequality and Foreign Aid in Retrospect' published in Pioneers in Development

4 T.W. Schultz: 'The Economics of Being Poor'

5 T.W. Schultz: Ibid

6 T.W. Schultz: Ibid

7 Amartya Sen: (1) Poverty and Famines: An Essay on Entitlement and Deprivation (2) Inequality Re-examined.

8 World Bank: World Development Report 1990-The estimate of poor people in the developing countries was based on a consumption based poverty line. It was estimated that all those who earned less than one dollar per day, will not be able to incur expenditure to buy minimum necessities of life.

9 World Social Summit-1995- Copenhagen: In March, 1995 the U.N. World Summit for Social Development took place in Copenhagen to address the issues of increasing ineaualities and widespread poverty. The summit was attended by representatives of 185 Governments and they committed themselves to the goal of eradicating poverty "as an ethical, social and political and moral imperative of humankind" and recognised people centered development as the key to achieve it.

10 There are variations in inter-state indicators of Human Development. For Kerala, state of India, the human indicators as given in original source are:

Life Expectancy	: 72.0
Infant mortality rate (*Per thousand births*) 1996	: 13
Adult Literacy rate (percent)	: 90

Kerala's performance is comparable with Asian Developing Countries such as China, Malaysia, Indonesia, Thailand etc.

Epilogue

In this book, we have travelled through memory lane where we came across streams of changing economic thought from classical to modern era. Ideas greatly impact the events and are also influenced by the latter. They clash and at times there are irreconcilable conflicts which generate enormous debate. For example, today, for economic prosperity, it is the integration with the global economy through the process of globalisation, that has become indispensable. Earlier, in the history of development thinking, some economists said that the dependence of developing countries on the developed countries is the main factor which causes underdevelopment. We have seen in the previous chapters that in the evolution of development thought and policy, a number of contradictions had emerged and were later, subjected to scrutiny through the compass of empirical evidence.

In recent years, debate on development thinking has been more pronounced between exponents of planned economy based on structuralist school of thought and exponents of open economy based on neoclassical resurgence. Both schools of thought provide guide posts which the policy makers have to apply in the task of development after taking into account the national characteristics of the economy and the stage of development achieved by it. Where the stage of the economic development is pre- take off, the role of public policy becomes predominant and opening up process has to be slow and cautious. In case of economies where there has been rapid industrialisation and the capacity to integrate with the world economy has been built up, free market forces can be allowed to play.

In this context, for further evolution of development thinking, the lessons of East Asia crisis of mid 1997 have added new dimensions. The East Asian crisis starting mid 1997 sharpened debate on the efficiency of market economy in meeting emerging challenges of developing countries. The main thrust in the policy-framework for development, following neoclassical resurgence was export led growth, and liberalisation of economies in both internal and external aspects. The East Asian Crisis raised the basic question whether liberalisation of economy was conducive to sustainable growth in view of slow down in the economic growth of Malaysia, Thailand, Indonesia and korea.

These countries had followed a policy of liberalisation which gave on average very high rate of growth in their G.D.P. since 1980s, low inflation rate and negligible unemployment. In the long run however some imbalances developed in these economies which finally led to crises in 1997. A large proportion of firms investing in these countries consisted of transnational firms which were engaged in exporting activities for foreign consumption. When there was a sluggish demand for their products, the production of the industries had to be curtailed. The other factor leading to imbalances in the economy was financing of deficit in the current account by short term capital inflows. The current account deficit of Malaysia for example stood at 5.9% of G.D.P. during 1995-97 which was very high. Reliance on short term capital to cover the current account deficit cannot be sustained in the long run because of volatile nature of this form of capital. Another imbalance in the economy developed from excessive growth in loans in the Banking sector. Most of these loans were given to unproductive sector viz. property sector. This led to resource misallocation. Since 1996 there was also sharp decline in foreign direct investment. This led to more and more demand for loans. At the same time because of recession, there was a credit squeeze in Japan. All these factors led to a situation when these countries accumulated much larger amount of short term debt which was larger than their foreign currency reserve.

The fact that the foreign debt was much more than foreign reserve, sent shockwaves throughout international markets. Towards the middle of 1997, because of continuous slowdown of exports and declining prices of the assets, the investors lost their confidence in the currencies and started withdrawing short term portfolio investment. This weakened the currencies of the region and led to further loss of confidence in the economy and that triggered off crisis in these economies.

One of the lessons of the East Asian crisis for developing countries is that economic openness especially the liberalisation of capital markets may be destablishing for these economies. In past, also when crisis occurred in Chilli in 1980s and in Mexico, in 1990s, these economies had adopted liberalisation programmes by adopting policies of free trade, privatisation, and deregulation which resulted in massive capital inflows into these economies and eventually the boom triggered a bust later. This led to a rapid outflow of capital and to subsequent economic slump. For the policy makers in the developing countries the repetition of financial crisis in East Asia deepened the fears that excessive and uncontrolled economic openness poses threats for economic growth.

The East Asian crisis however does not imply the retreat to economic isolation. Recent global economic developments have increased the need for greater interdependence. There are certain benefits from the globalisation namely enhanced comparative advantage in terms of trade, opportunities to channel excess global capital into developing economies in the form of foreign direct investment and opportunities for foreign technology transfer. Economic openners has become an integral part of development process. However in implementation of liberalisation programmes caution has to be exercised by the developing country because economic openness increases vulnerability to external forces. The policies have to be designed to keep the degree of vulnerability to the minimum by a skilful management of the macro economy.

The lesson therefore of East Asian crisis is that liberalisation should be effected in various stages. Indian approach to capital account liberalisation can be emulated by the developing countries. Caution should be also exercised that in the process of liberalisation, macro economic fundamentals should remain sound such as current account deficit and G.D.P ratio and debt service ratio etc. The policy of credit channelled through banking sector also need continuous scrutiny so that productive sector is not ignored. There should be also adequate checks and balances on the flow of short term capital for which reserve requirements may be necessary.

In past, we have seen that development thought in various stages passed through critical assessment whenever there was a gap between the global economic development and existing ideas. This happened when classical and neoclassical postulates were challenged by keynes in order to find out a cure for great depression in 1930s. This again happened when during postwar era development economics was born to address problems of underdevelopment and poverty which could not be effectively tackled by classical, neoclassical and keynesian theories. There was then a counter-revolution in the form of neoclassical resurgence in 1970s and 1980s. The events of 1990s, especially after East Asian crisis further brought to focus the gap between the development policies based on neoclassical resurgence and the objectives of sustained economic development.

The analysis of growth experience has shown that because of widening income gap, convergence of the developing countries with the developed countries has been very slow and limited to some successful East Asian countries. The East Asian crisis has deepened the concern further because there is a danger that trend towards convergence may be reversed. The growth melt-down in the East Asian countries, affected by the crisis has also resulted in a set back to the spectacular achievement in poverty alleviation both in terms of income poverty and in terms of human poverty. According to some estimate, the proportion of the Indonesian population living on income below the poverty line in 1998, was expected to be at least 50% greater than in 1996. Similarly poverty in Thailand is expected to increase by at least one third. The crisis has also resulted in increase in the rate of unemployment. Out of the countries affected by the crisis viz. Malaysia, Thailand, Indonesia and Republic of Korea, greatest increase in unemployment and poverty is expected to occur in Indonesia. In Thailand, unemployment rose from 5.4% of the labour force in 1997 to 8.8% in February 1998. Unemployment in Korea also has increased.

The East Asian debacle thus presents new challenges for development thought and policy. These economies succeeded in combining rapid economic growth with spectacular improvement in education, life expectancy, health care and eradication of poverty. The crisis has now impinged on the success of these economies in achieving growth and also in giving human face to development which is the most important imperative in modern development thinking. The intellectual challenge then is how to build up the basis for sustained growth for developing countries so that the dividends of economic growth in terms of eradication of poverty and "catching up" are not lost. One of the new areas in which development economics has to probe will be how to mitigate the negative effects of economic crisis on poor and less advantaged part of the society. Equally important for future direction of development economics will be to build up an analytical framework which will support the policy makers in providing important checks and balance to the operation of market forces in developing economies.

To sum up, in its further evolution, the development economics faces threefold challenges. These include the following:

i) To build up a suitable theoretical framework within which development policies are reoriented towards narrowing the development gap.

ii) For an urgent attack on widespread poverty, foundations for economics of poverty need to be laid down. This will generate much needed thrust and shift in development policy.

iii) In the context of East Asian crisis, there is a need for innovations of new mechanisms which can counter setback to growth. Conceptual advance in development economies is needed to analyse the factors which slowed down the rapid convergence of East Asian Countries in recent past.

References

Chapter II

ABRAMOVITZ MOSES 1989: Thinking about Growth Cambridge University Press-Cambridge.

ARNDT H.W. 1978: The Rise and Fall of Economic Growth-Longman Chesire Melbourne

BARAN PAUL 1957: The Political Economy of Growth-Monthly Review Press, New York.

BHARADWAJ KRISHNA 1989: Themes in Value and Distribution-Classical theory reappraisal-Unwin Hyman Ltd. 15/17, Broadvick Street, London.

BLAUG MARK 1985: Economic theory in Retrospect Cambridge University Press, Cambridge, New Yrok-4th edition, New Rochelle.

BLAUG MARK 1986: Economic History and the History of Economics, New York University Press-Washington, Square, New York.

CHENERY H. AND SRINIVASAN T.N. 1968 (ED.): Handbook of Development Economics Vol. I: Amsterdam North Holland Press.

CLARK COLIN 1984: Development Economics: The Early Years, in Gerald M Meier and Dudley Seers (ed)-Pioneers in Development-Oxford University Press, New York.

COLE CHARLES L. 1969: The Economic Fabric of Society-Harcourt, Brace & World Inc, New York-Chicago.

FUSFELD DANIEL R 1981: The Age of the Economist-Scott, Foresman and Company-Glenview, Illionis.

GREENAWAY DAVID, BLEONEY MICHAEL AND STEWARD IANHT 1981: Companion to Contemporary Economic Thought-Routledge-London and New York.

LITTLE, I.M.D. 1982: Economic Development: Theory, Policy and International Relations-Basic Books, New York.

MEIER G.M. and R.E. BALDWIN 1957: Economic Development: Theory, History, Policy, Wiley, New Work.

MEIER GERALD M. AND DUDLEY SEERS (Eds) 1984: Pioneers in Development-Oxford University Press-New York.

MEIER GERALD. M. 1989: Leading Issues in Economic Development: Oxford University Press, New York.

O'BRIEN, D.P. 1975: The classical Economists-Clarendon Press-Oxford.

ROLL ERIC 1975: A History of Economic Thought-Oxford University Press, Delhi.

ROSTOW W.W 1990: Theorists of Economic Growth-From David Hume to the Present-Oxford University Press, New York: Oxford.

SAVIN DAVOR: Keynes and the Development of unemployment theory in 'Development cooperation N.22 June '96 published from Republic of Slovania.

SCHUMPETER JOSEPH A. 1934: The Theory of Economic Development-Harvard University Press-Cambridge, Mass.

SINGER H.W.1964: The Mechanics of Economic Development-Mcgrow Hill, New York.

STREETEN PAUL 1979: 'Development Ideas in Perspective' in Towards a New Strategy for Development-A Rothko Chapel Collaguiem.

STREETEN PAUL 1984: 'Postscript: Development Dichotomies' in Pioneers in Development (eds) G.M. Meier and Dudely Seers.

THIRLWALL A.P. (ED.): Keynes and Economic Development Seventh Keynes Seminar 1985

THIRLWALL A.P.: Macro Economic Issues from a Keynesian Perspective.

Chapter III

ABRAMOVITZ MOSES 1991: Thinking About Growth-Cambridge University Press-Cambridge-New York.

ADELMAN IRMA 1961: Theories of Economic Growth and Development , Stanford University, Stanford.

ADELMAN AND E THORBECKE (ED.) 1966: The Theory and Design of Economic Development-Baltimore and London, John Hopkins Press.

ARNDT H.W. 1978: The Rise and Fall of Economic Growth-Longman Cheshire-Melbourne.

ARNDT H.W. 1987: Economic Development`university of Chicago Press Chicago.

ATTIYEH RICHARD, LUMSDEN KEITH AND BACH GEORGE BLAND 1970: Macro Economics-A Programmed Book-Prentice Hall-Inc-Englewood Cliffe New York.

BALOGH THOMAS, 1964: Unequal Partners, Basil Blackwell, Oxford, England.

BAUER P.T. & YAMEY B.S., 1957: The Economics of Under Developed Countries, university of Chicago Press, Chicago.

BAUER P.T. 1971: Dissent on Development-Widenfield and Nicholsan-London.

BRENER Y.S. 1966: Theories of Economic Development and Growth-George Allen Unwin Ltd. London.

BRUTON HENREY J, 1965: Principles of Development Economics-Prentice-Hall, INC, Engglewood G Cliffs, New York.

CAIRNCROSS A.K. 1962: Factors in Economic Development, George Allen, UNWIN. London.

CHENERY H. & STRINIVASAN T.N. (EDS.), 1989: Handbook of Development Economics Amsterdan-North Holland.

CHENERY H. 1979: Structural Change and Development Policy-Oxford University Press-London.

COLE KEN, CAMERON JOHN and EDWARDS CHRIS, 1983: Why Economists Disagree-The Political economy of Economics-Longman, London and New York.

EICHNER ALFRED S (ED): A Guide to Post Keynesian Economics-M.E. Shape, Inc., White Plains, New York.

ENKE STEPHEN 1964: Economics for Development-Dennis Dobson.

FRANK A. 1978: Dependent Accumulation and underdevelopment-Macmillan.

GERALD M MEIR (Ed.), 1984: Pioneers in Development-Second Series, World bank.

GERSCHENKRON ALEXANDER 1962: Economic Backwardness in Historical Perspective: Cambridge, Mass: Harvard University Press.

GERSOVILZ MARK (Ed.), 1983: The Theory and Experience of Economic Development Essays in honour of Sir W.A. Lewis, George Allen and Unwin, London.

GILLIS MALCOLM, PERKINS DWIGHT H, REOMER MICHAEL AND SHODGRASS DONALD R 1987: Economics of Development-W.W. Norton & Company, New York, London.

GOULD J.D., 1972: Economic Growth in History-Methueux Co. Ltd., London.

HIGGINS B 1959 (Revised) 1963: Economic Development, Principles, Problems and Policies, New York: Norton.

HIRSCHMAN A.O, 1981: 'The Rise and Decline of Development Economics' in A.O. Hirschman's essays in Trespassing-Cambridge University Press, Cambridge.

HIRSCHMAN A.O., 1958: Strategy of Economic Development-New Haven Yale University Press.

HOSELITZ BERT F 1960: Sociological Aspects of Economic Growth (Glencoo Ill: The Free Press).

HUNT DIANNA: Economic theories of Development-Savage M.D. Barnes and Noble Books, School of African and Asian Studies, University of Sussex.

KUHN W.E. PHD 1963: Evolution of Economic thought-South Western Publishing Company-Chicago-44.

KUZNETS, S 1966: Modern Economic Growth: New Haven-Yale University Press.

LEIBENSTEIN H, 1957: Economic Backwardness and Economic Growth, Wiley, New York.

LEWIS W.A. 1955: The Theory of Economic Growth-Allen and Unwin-London.

LITTLE I.M.D., 1982: Economic Development: Theory, Policy and International Relations-Basic Books, New York.

MEIER GERALD M 1989: Leading Issues in Economic Development-Oxford University Press, Oxford.

MYINT HLA, 1964: The Economics of Underdeveloped Countries-Hutchinsan, London.

MYRDAL GUNNAR 1957: Economic Theory and Underdeveloped Region-Duckworth London.

MYRDAL GUNNAR 1968: Asian Drama-Random House-New York.

MEIER G.M. & BALDWIN R.E. 1957: Economic Development: Theory, History, Policy, Wiley: New York.

NELSON EASTIN (ED.), 1960: Economic Growth-Proceedings of the Conference on Economic Development sponsored by the Department of Economics and the Institute of Latin American Economics at the University of Texas-University of Texas Press, Austin.

NELSON EASTIN (EDT) 1960: Economic Growth-University of Texas Press Austin.

NORMAN GEMMELL, 1987: Surveys in Development Economics-Basic Blackwell.

NURKSE R 1953: Problems of Capital Formation in Underdeveloped countries-Oxford University Press-New York.

O' BRIEN D.P. 1975: The classical Economists-Oxford, Clarendon Press.

RIMA I.H. 1967: Development of Economic Analysis-Richard D. Irwin, Inc. Homewood, Illionis.

ROBBINS L. 1968-The Theory of Economic Development in the History of Economic thought Macmillan.

RODAN PAUL ROSENTEEIN, 1963: Problems of Industrialisation of Eastern and South Eastern Europe-The Economics of Under development reprint in A.N. Agarwal and S.P. Singh ed., Oxford University Press, New York.

ROSTOW W.W. 1990: Theorists of Economic Growth from David Hume to present: Oxford University Press.

ROSTOW W.W., 1960: The Stages of Economic Growth-Cambridge University Press.

SCHUMPETER J.A. 1934: The Theory of Economic Development-Harvard University Press-Cambridge.

SINGER H.W. 1964: International Development: Growth and Change McGraw Hill, New York.

STREETEN P. "Development Ideas in Historical Perspectives in Development Perspectives (Ed.) reprinted in Pioneers in Development (Ed.) Meier G. and Seers D. (Oxford 1984).

THIRLWALL A P, 1989: Growth and Development, Macmillan Education, ltd.

TINBERGEN J 1958: The Design of Development John Hopkins Press, Baltimore.

CHAPTER IV

ABRAMOVITZ MOSES, 1990: Thinking about Growth-Cambridge University Press.

ARIFF MOHAMMED & HILL HAL, 1985: Export Oriented Industrialisation-The Asean Experience-Allen and Unwin-Sydney, London, Boston.

ASIAN DEVELOPMENT BANK, 1997: Emerging Asia-Changes and Challenges-ADB, Manila.

ASIAN DEVELOPMENT BANK: Asian Development Outlook (1993-97)-ADB, Manila.

BRANDT REPORT, 1980: North-South-A Programme for Survival.

CHENERY HOLLIS, 1974: Structural Change and Development Policy, Oxford University Press, London.

CHENERY HOLLIS & SYRQUIN MOISES, 1975: Patterns of Development (1950-70)-Oxford University Press, London.

CULPEPER ROY, BERRY ALBERT & STEWART FRANCES 1997: Global Development fifty years after Bretton Woods (Essays in honour of Gerald K Helleiner), The North-South Institute.

EXPORT-IMPORT BANK OF INDIA, 1995: Some Aspects of International Debt of Developing Countries-October 1995.

FOREIGN AFFAIRS: Globalising Free Trade (C. Fred Bergsten) Foreign Affairs May-June 1996.

FORSTNER HELMUT & BALANCE ROBERT, 1990: Competing in a Global Eonomy, Prepared for the UNIDO, London Unwin Hyman.

GRABOSKI RICHARD and SCHILDS MICHAEL: Development Economics, Blackwell Publishers Cambridge, USA.

HANSSON GOTE, 1991: Trade, Growth and Development, Routelage, London.

HELLEINER G.K.: The New Global Economy and the Developing Countries.

HETTNE BJORN, 1990: Development Theory and the Three Worlds-Longman, Scientific & Technical, London.

INTERNATIONAL LABOUR REVIEW ARTICLE: Globalisation and Employment-International Labour Review Vol. 135.

KRUEGER ANNE O, 1985: Development with Trade-LDCs and the International Economy-Institute for Contemporary Studies, San Francisco.

KRUEGER ANNE O, 1990: Perspectives on Trade and Development, Harvester Wheatsheaf New York.

KRUGMAN PAUL R., 1990: Rethinking International Trade-The MIT Press, Cambridge.

KRUGMAN PAUL, 1994: The myth of Asia's Miracle-Foreign Affairs, November-December.

KRUGMAN PAUL, 1997: Is capitalism too productive-Foreign Affairs September October 1997.

LAWRENCE ROBERT Z, 1996: The slow growth Mystery-Foreign Affairs-January-February 1996.

LEWIS W.A., 1980: Article-The Slowing Down of the Engine of Growth-American Economic Review-September 1980.

LEWIS W.A., 1964: Employment Policy in Underdeveloped Areas-1958, Reprinted in G.M. Meier-Leading Issues in Economic Development-Oxford University Press.

MARTIN KURT, 1990: Strategies of Economic Development: Institute of Social Studies, Macmillan Academic and Professional Ltd., London.

MEIER G, 1963: International Trade and Development-Harper and Row, New York.

MEIER G, 1970 (Ed): Leading issues in Development Economics-Oxford University Press, New York.

MITLEMAN JAMES H: Globalisation-Critical reflection Rienner publisher, INC, USA.

MYRDAL GUNNAR, 1956: Asian Drama-Random House, New York.

NANCY BIRDSALE, DAVID ROSS, RICHARD SABOT: Inequality and Growth reconsiderd: Lessons from East Asia-The World Bank Economic Review, September 1995, New York.

NARAYHAN EDUDAN: Privatisation strategies in Developing Countries-Economic and Political Weekly July 5, 1997.

PEARSON REPORT, 1969: Partners in Development-Report of the Commission on International Development-Pall Mall Press.

POMFRET RICHARD, 1991: International Trade, Basil Blackwell.

QUIBRIA M.G. (Ed.) 1994: Rural Poverty in Developing Asia-Asian Development Bank, Manila.

RONALD W JONES & KRUEGER ANNE O (Ed.): The political economy of International Trade-Essays in Honour of Robert E. Bal Dwin.

SAVRIC J, BRECHER IRVING: Equity and efficiency in economic development (Essay in honour of Bengamin Higgins), Intermediate Technology.

SCHULTZ THEODORE W., 1993: The Economics of Being Poor-Blackwell Publishers, Cambridge, USA.

SCOTT MAURICE FITZERALD, 1989: A New View of Economic Growth-Clerenden Press, Oxford.

SEHASTIAN EDWARD: Latin America's Under performance Vol. 76, Foreign Affairs, March-April 1997.

SELIGSON MITCHELL A. and PASSELSMITH JOHN T., 1993: Development & Underdevelopment (ed): Lynne Rienner Publishers INC, USA.

SINGER HANS W & ANSARI J.A., 1988: Rich and Poor Countries-UNWIN Hyman, London.

SINGH AJIT, 1995: How did East Asia Grow so fast-Discussion paper-UNCTAD February 1995.

STREETEN PAUL, 1981: First Things First-Meeting Basic Human Needs in the Developing Countries-Oxford University Press.

STREETEN PAUL, 1989: Mobilising Human Potential-The Challenge of Unemployment-UNDP.

TAYLOR LANCE, 1993: The Rocky Road to Reform-The United Nations University, Wider-Tokyo.

THE ECONOMIST: A Survey of China-March 1995.

THE ECONOMIST: A Survey of Mexico-The Economist October 1995.

THE ECONOMIST: A Survey of the World Economy-The Economist, 28th September 1996.

TOYE JOHN, 1995: Structural Adjustment and Employment Policy-I.L.O, Geneva.

U.N. GENERAL ASSEMBLY: Report of the Secretary General on Implementation of the International Development Strategy for the Fourth U.N. Development Decade, 1992-A/47/270-E/1992/74 dated 18th June 1992.

U.N.G.A. 45TH REPORT: The challenge to the South-Report by Group of 77.

UNCTAD REVIEW, 1994: U.N. New York.

UNCTAD: The Least Developed Countries Report 1990-98.

UNITED NATIONS, 1993: Report on the World Social Situation-U.N. 1993, New York.

UNITED NATIONS, 1995: The Copen-Hagen Declaration and programme of Action-World Summary for Social Development 1995, U.N. New York.

UNITED NATIONS: Proceedings of the UNCTAD: 7th Session-Geneva 9th July to 3rd August 1987-Volume III-Basic Documents.

UNITED NATIONS: World Economic and Social Survey (1995-98).

WILBER CHARLES K., JAMESON KENNETH P.,: An Inquiry into the poverty of Economics, university of Notredame Press, Notredame and London.

WORLD BANK, 1993: The East Asian Mircale-A World Bank Policy Research Paper-Oxford University Press.

WORLD BANK: Development priorities for 1990s staff paper by Economic Adviser Policy & Review Department.

WORLD BANK: The World Bank Economic Review January 1997.

WORLD BANK: The World Bank Economic Review-January 1996-Volume 10-N.I.

WORLD BANK: World Development Report, Oxford University Press, New York-Several issues.

WORLD LABOUR REPORT, 1995: I.L.O. Geneva 1995.

CHAPTER V

ADELMAN & THORBECK (Ed.) 1966: The Theory and Design of Economic Development-John Hopkin Press-Baltimore.

BALASSA BELA, 1989: New Directions in the World Economy-MacMillan, London.

BALASUBRAMANIAM & LALL SANJAY (Ed.): Current Issues in Development Economics.

CAIRNCROSS ALEC & PURI MOHINDER, 1976: Employment, Income Distribution and Development Strategy-The Mcmillan press Ltd.

CHOKSI AMERE M & DEMETRIS PAPAGEORION, 1986: Economic Liberalisation in developing countries, Basil Blackwell.

CLINE WILLIAM R & WENTRAUB SYDNEY (Ed.), 1981: Economic Stabilisation in Developing Countries-The Brishings Institutions, Washington.

CULPEPER ROY, BERRY ALBERT & STEWART FRANCES (Ed.) 1983: Global Development Fifty Years after Brettan Woods-The North South Institute-MacMillan Press ltd., London.

DREZE JEAN AND SEN AMARTYA: 1989 Hunger and Public Action: Clarendon Press , Oxford.

EDOHO FELIX MOSES, 1997: Globalisation and the World Order-Praeger London.

EDWARD EDGAR O (Ed.), 1974: Employment in Developing Nations-Report on a Ford Foundation Study, Columbia University Press.

FUKUYAMA FRANCIS, 1995: Social Capital & the Global Economy in Foreign Affairs, September/October 1995.

GALBRAITH JOHN KENNETH, 1958: The Affluent Society-Houguton Miffin Boston.

GEMEL NORMAL (Ed.), 1997: Survey in Development Economics-Basil Blackwell.

GOVERNMENT OF INDIA: Economic Survey 1996-97, 1997-98, 1998-99.

GOVT. OF INDIA: National Sample Survey Report 1993-Government of India Publications.

GWYWNE ROBERT N, 1990: New Horizons-Third World Industrialisation in an International Framework-London Scientific and Technical, London.

HEGGARD STEPHEN, 1989: Article 'The East Asian NICS in Comparative Pespectives-Annals-Aapss.

HETTNE BIORN, 1990: Development Theory and the Three Worlds-Layman-Scientific and Technilca, London.

IMF: World Economic Outlook Several issues, IMF Washington.

JOBERTO ALEX E FERNANDEX & MONEMEN ANDRE (Ed.), 1996: Liberalisation in the Developing World-Routedge, London and New York.

LARUE C. STEVEN, DEARBORN FITZROY (Ed.), 1995: The Indian Handbook-The World Bank.

MEIER GERALD M (Ed.), 1987: Pioneers in Development –Second Series-Oxford University Press.

MEIER GERALD M & SEERS DUDLEY (Ed.), 1984: Pioneers in Development first Series, Oxford University Press, New York.

MINISTRY OF AGRICULTURE, 1983: Report of the Committee to Review the Existing Administrative arrangements for rural Developments and Poverty Alleviation Programme-Department of Rural Development.

MYRDAL GUNNAR, 1970: The Challenge of World Poverty-Allen Lane-The Penguin Press, London.

NAGRAJ R., 1997: What has happened since 1991?: Assessment of India's Reform-Economy and Political Weekly, No. 8, 1997.

P.R. BRAHMANANDA: Amartya Sen and Welfare Economics, Sudha Publications, Bangalore.

PATEL I.G., 1992: Policies for African Development (Ed.): IMF, Washington.

PLANNING COMMISSION, 1993: Report of the Expert Group on Estimation of Proportion and Number of Poor People-Planning Commission, Government of India, New Delhi.

PLANNING COMMISSION: Ninth Five Year Plan-Government of India Publicatiaons.

PRICHETT LANT, 1997: Divergence Big Time-Journal of Economic Perspectives Vol. II, No. 3-Summer 1997.

RANIS GUSTAV & SCHULTZ PAUL T (Ed.) 1989: The State of Development Economics-Basil lackwell, Cambridge Centre, Cambridge.

RONALD W JONES & KRUEGER ANNE O (Ed), 1986: The political Economy of International Trade Basil Blackwell, Cambridge.

SACHS JAFFREY, 1996: Growth in Africa-The Economist-June 29, 1996

SAVIRE DONALD J & PRECHER IRVIN G (Ed.), 1992: Equality and Efficiency in Economic Development. Intermediate Technology Publications.

SCHUMACHER ERNEST FRIEDRICK, 1973: Small is Beautiful.

SCOTT MAURICE FITZERALD, 1989: A new View of Economic Growth-Clerendan Press-Oxford.

SEN & DREZE, 1995: India-Economic Development and Social Opportunity-Oxford University Press, Delhi.

SEN, AMARTYA 1982: Poverty and Famines: An Essay on Entitlement and Deprivation Oxford: Clarendon Press.

SEN, AMARTYA, 1983: Development-Which Way Now? Economic Journal 93: 745-62.

SEN, AMARTYA, 1994: Resources, Values and Development. Oxford: Basil Blackwell.

STREETEN PAUL, 1989: Mobilising Human potential-The Challenge of Unemployment-UNDP., New York.

STREETEN PAUL, 1996: Adjustments Globalisation and Social Development in Development and International Cooperation Journal, Vol. XII, New York-June 1996.

TAYLER LANCE (Ed), 1993: The Rocky Road to Reforms-The U.N. University, Tokyo.

THEPHAS CAROLINS & WILKIN PETER (Ed.), 1997: Globalisation and the South-Mao Millen Press Ltd., London.

THOMAS CAROLINE, WILKIN PETER, 1997: Globalisation and the South-Macmillan Press Ltd., London.

UNCTAD: Accelerating the Development Process-Challenges for National and International Policies in 1990s-TD/354/Rev.

UNCTAD: The Current World Economics Crisis and Perspectives for the 1990s-Report by UNCTAD Sectt. 1993-TD/272 and Addl.

UNCTAD: Trade and Development Report several issues UNCTAD, Palais des Nations, Geneva.

UNDP: Human Development Report-Several issues. Oxford University Press, London.

UNDP: Human Development Report-South Asia 1997 Oxford University Press, London.

UNITED NATIONS: World Economic and Social Survey several issues.

WORLD BANK, 1993: Implementing the World Bank's Strategy to reduce poverty-Progress & Challenges-World Bank Staff Papers.

WORLD BANK: Global Economic Prospects and Developing Countries several issues.